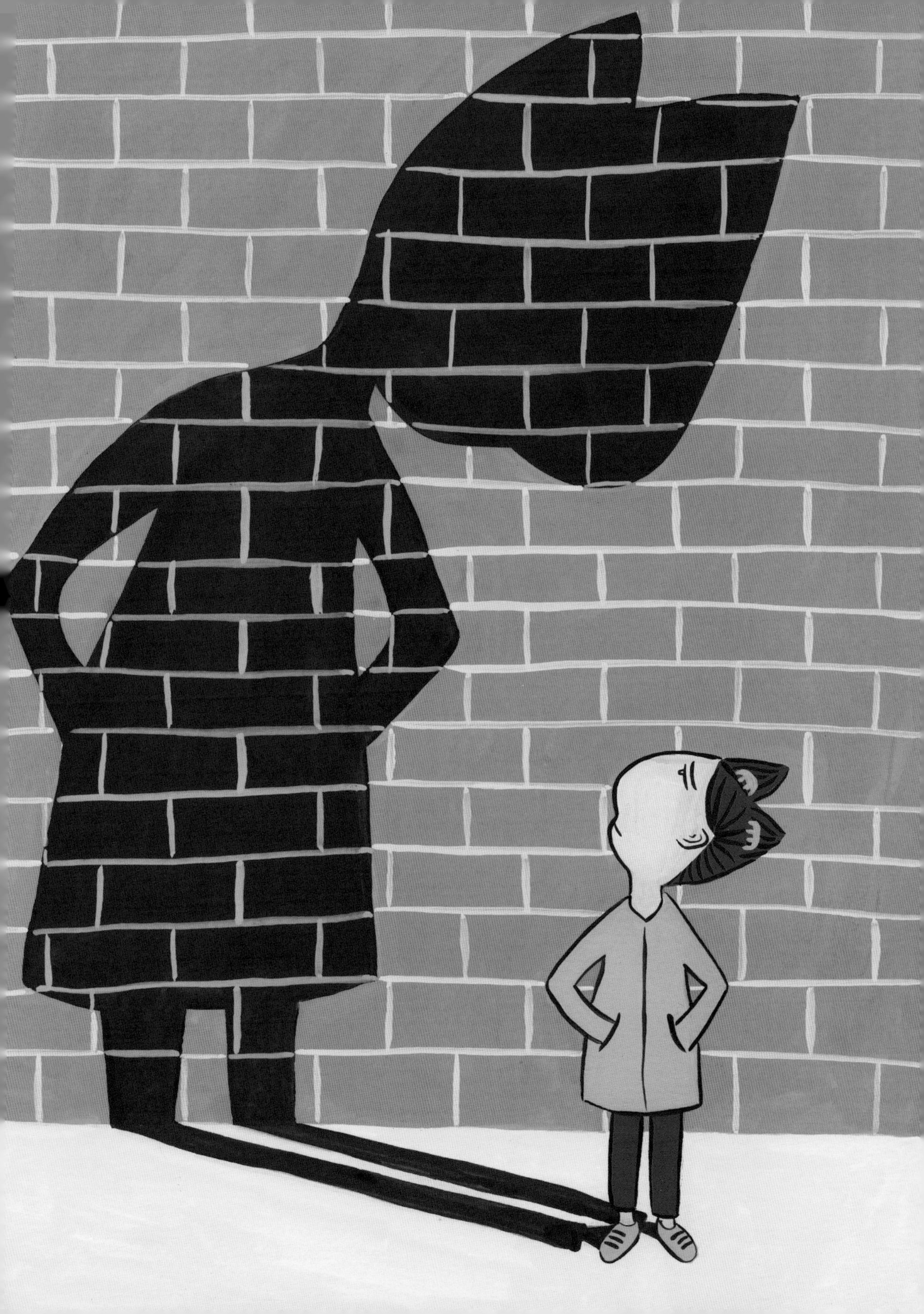

A Firefly Book

Published under license from the National Film Board of Canada by Firefly Books Ltd. 2018
Book design and adaptation © 2018 Firefly Books Ltd.
Text and illustrations © 2018 Andrea Dorfman
Adapted from the film *Flawed* © National Film Board of Canada, 2010

First printing

Library of Congress Control Number: 2018932205

Library and Archives Canada Cataloguing in Publication
Dorfman, Andrea, author, illustrator
Flawed / by Andrea Dorfman.
(National Film Board of Canada collection)
Adapted from the film Flawed.
ISBN 978-0-228-10071-3 (hardcover)
1. Dorfman, Andrea. 2. Dorfman, Andrea--Pictorial works.
3. Self-acceptance. 4. Self-acceptance--Pictorial works. 5. Self-perception. 6. Self-perception--Pictorial works. 7. Body image.
8. Body image--Pictorial works. 9. Surgery, Plastic--Popular works. 10. Surgery, Plastic--Pictorial works. I. Title. II. Title:
Flawed (Motion picture)
BF575.S37D67 2018   158.1   C2018-900611-0

Published in the United States by
Firefly Books (U.S.) Inc.
P.O. Box 1338, Ellicott Station
Buffalo, New York 14205

Published in Canada by
Firefly Books Ltd.
50 Staples Avenue, Unit 1
Richmond Hill, Ontario L4B 0A7

Cover and interior design: Hartley Millson

Printed in China

 We acknowledge the financial support of the Government of Canada.

The NFB is Canada's public producer of award-winning creative documentaries, auteur animation, interactive stories and participatory experiences. NFB producers are embedded in communities across the country, from St. John's to Vancouver, working with talented creators on innovative and socially relevant projects. The NFB is a leader in gender equity in film and digital media production, and is working to strengthen Indigenous-led production, guided by the recommendations of Canada's Truth and Reconciliation Commission. NFB productions have won over 7,000 awards, including 18 Canadian Screen Awards, 17 Webbys, 12 Oscars and more than 100 Genies. To access NFB works, visit NFB.ca or download our apps for mobile devices

FLAWED

A Story By
Andrea Dorfman

National Film Board of Canada Collection

FIREFLY BOOKS

His name is Dave and he's a plastic surgeon.

Even though my friends told me he was the nicest guy in the world, I decided I didn't like him. I thought plastic surgery made people feel flawed.

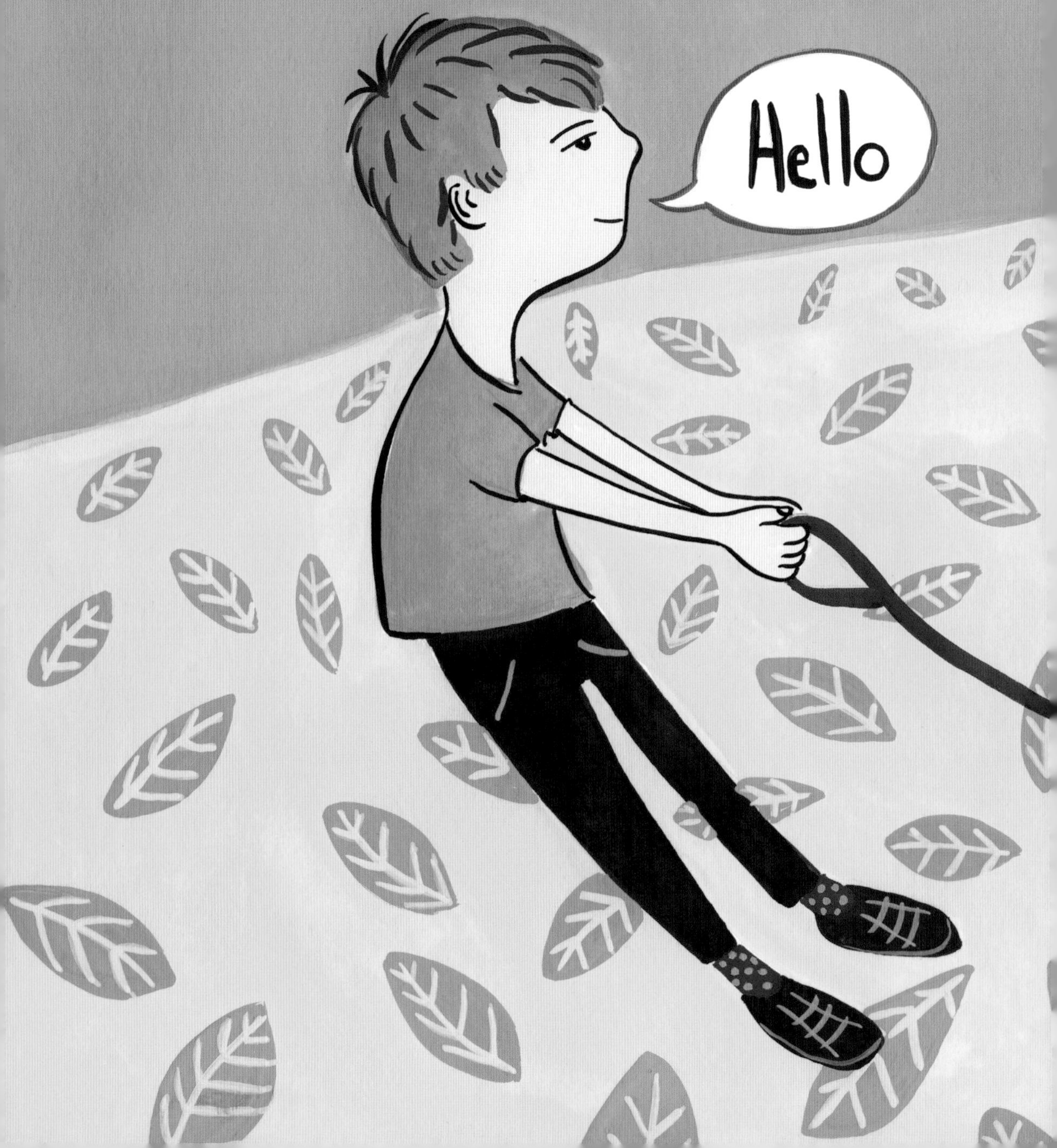
Hello

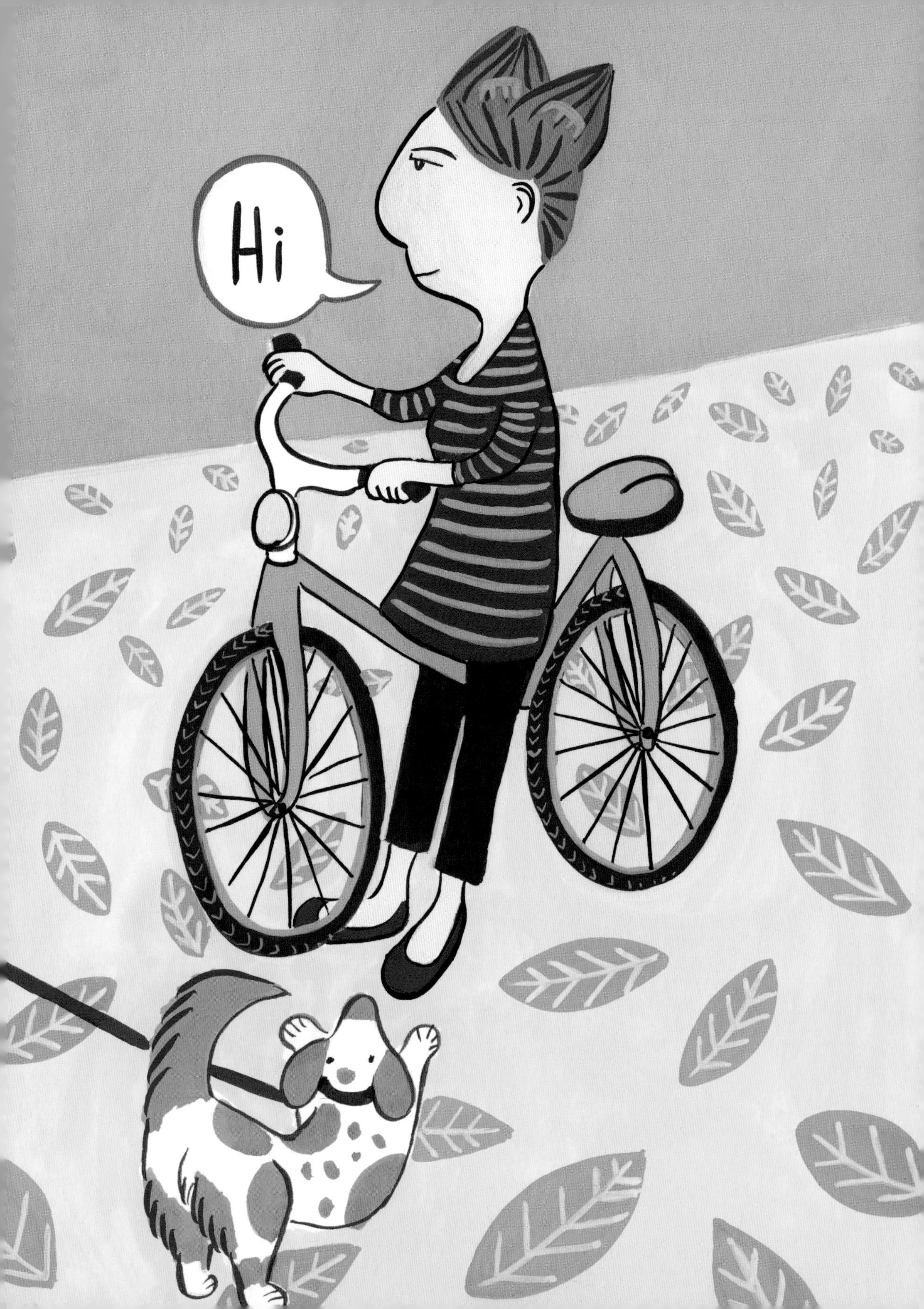
Hi

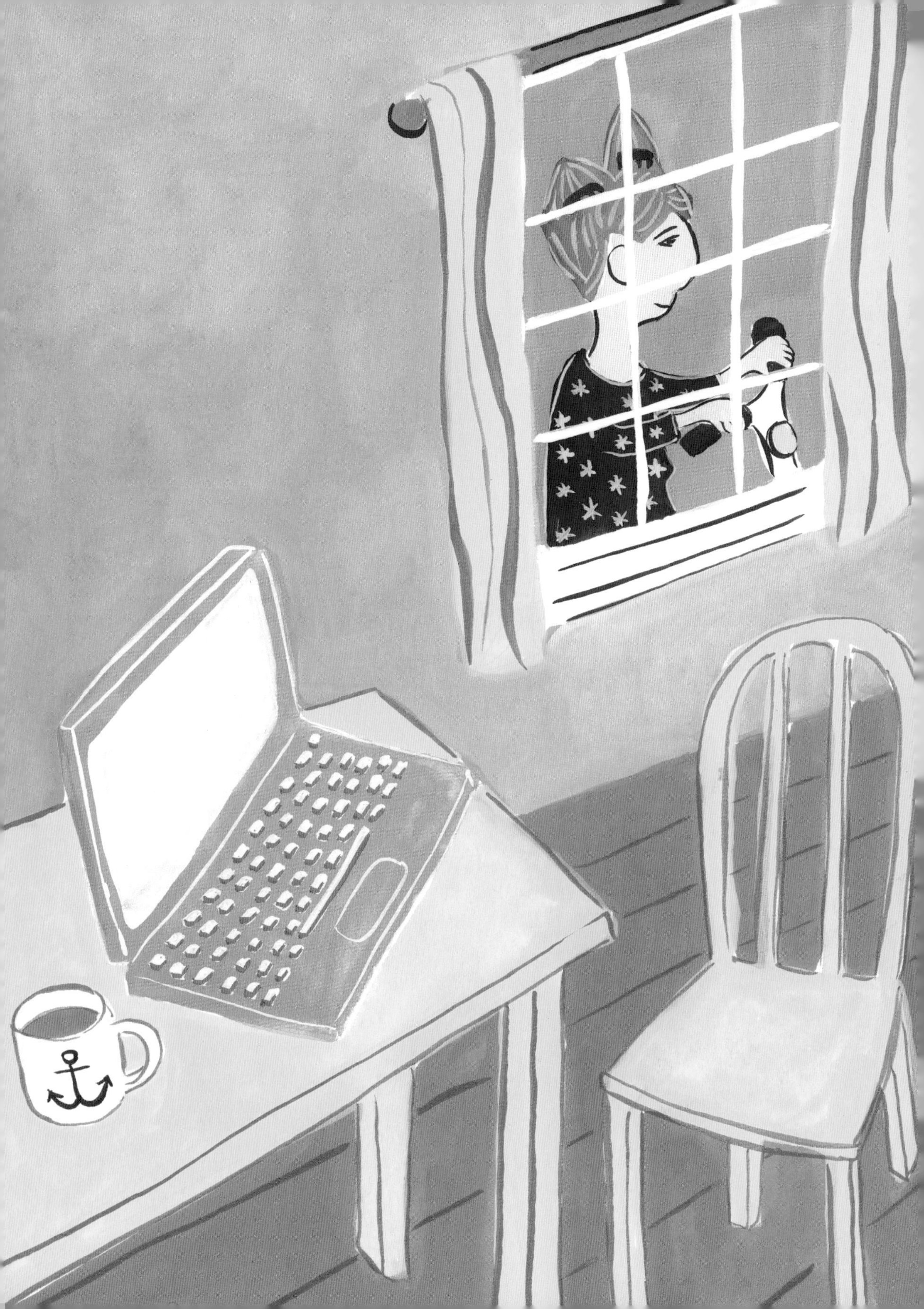

We first met in Halifax.

I was there for the summer, housesitting for a friend. I was also writing a film script — or at least trying to. There were lots of distractions: old friends, concerts, the ocean ... and Dave.

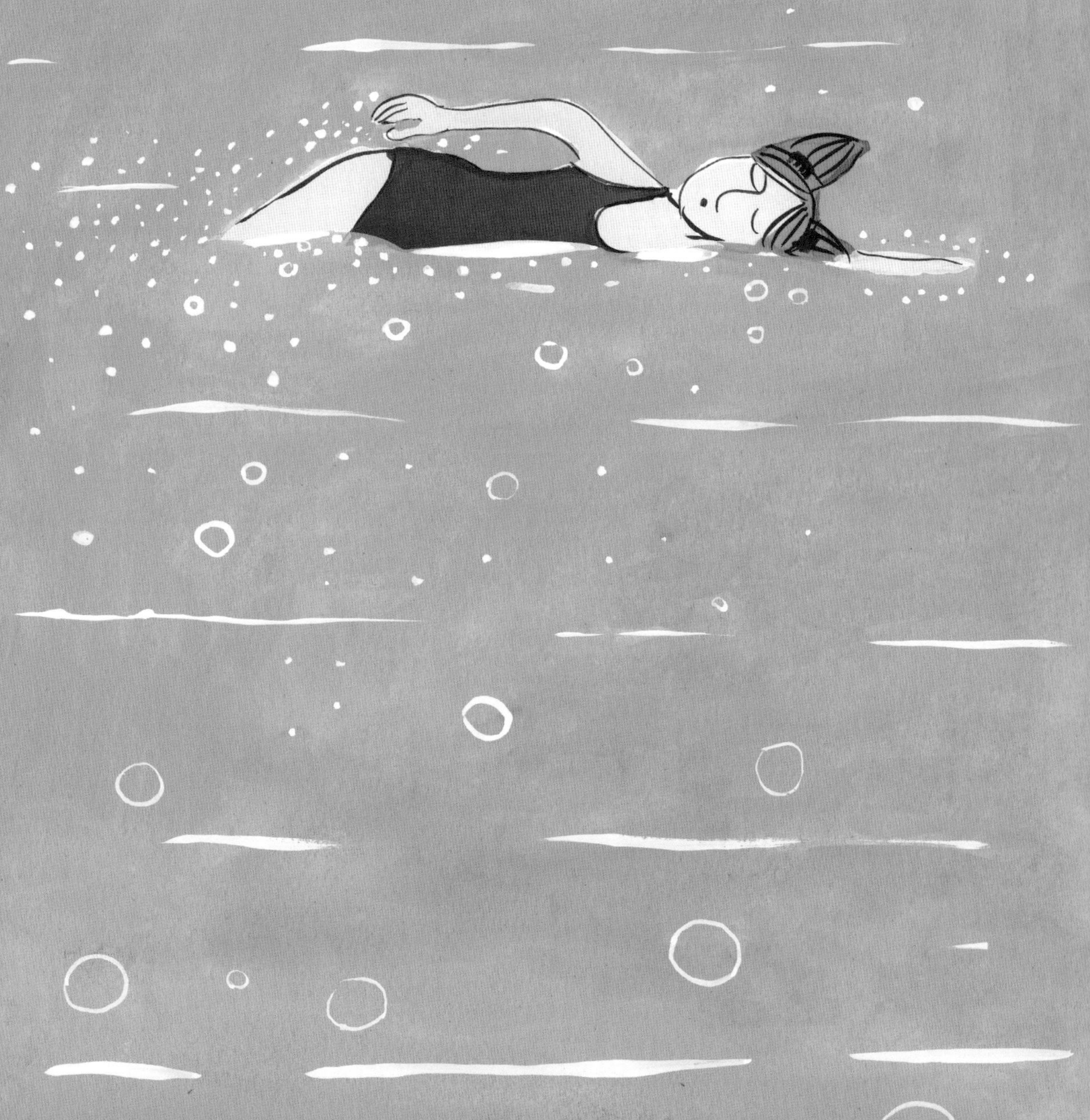

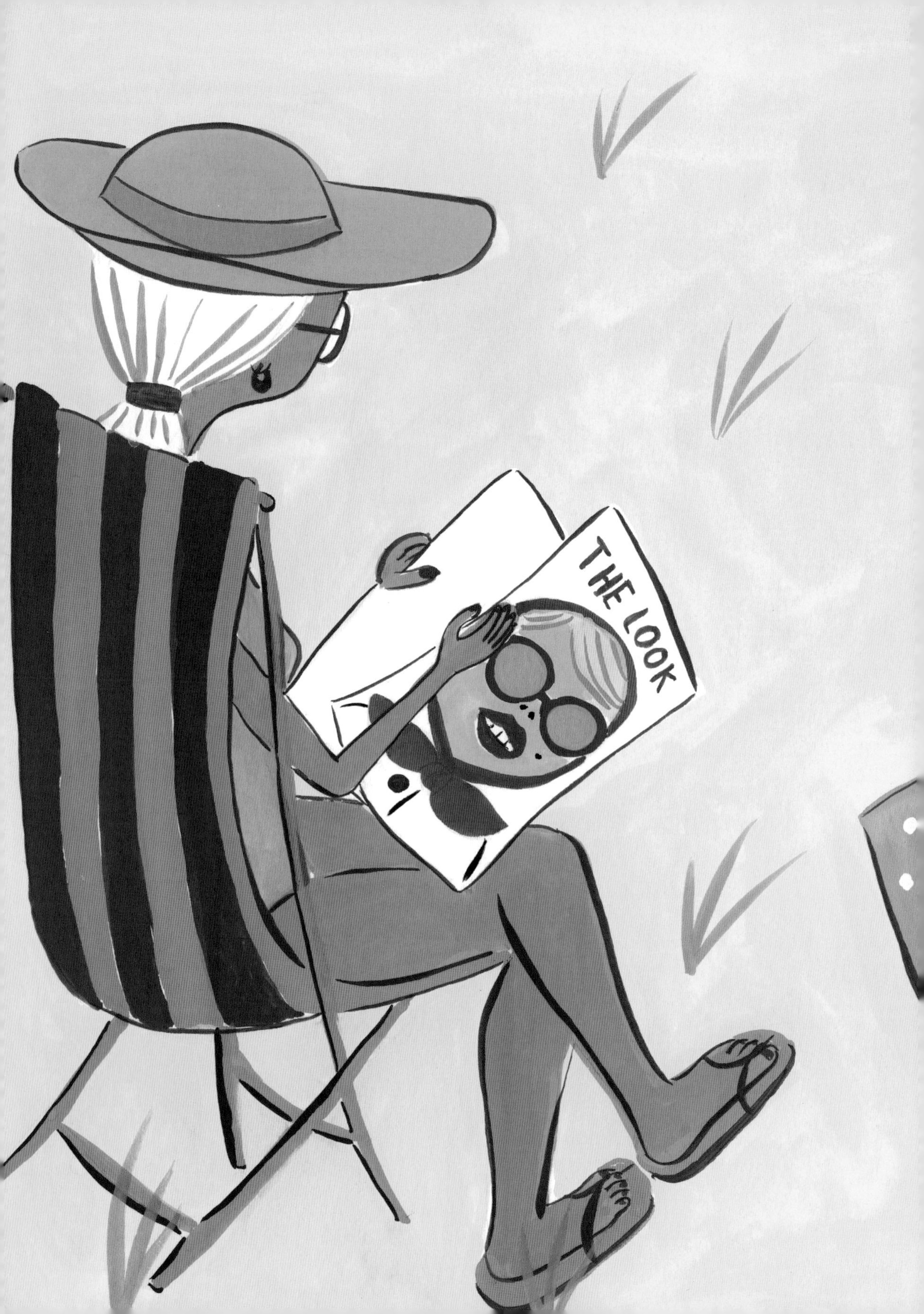
THE LOOK

Dave was a conundrum. The fact that his job was to operate on perfectly healthy people in an attempt to make them "beautiful" bothered me so much, I wondered if we could ever be friends.

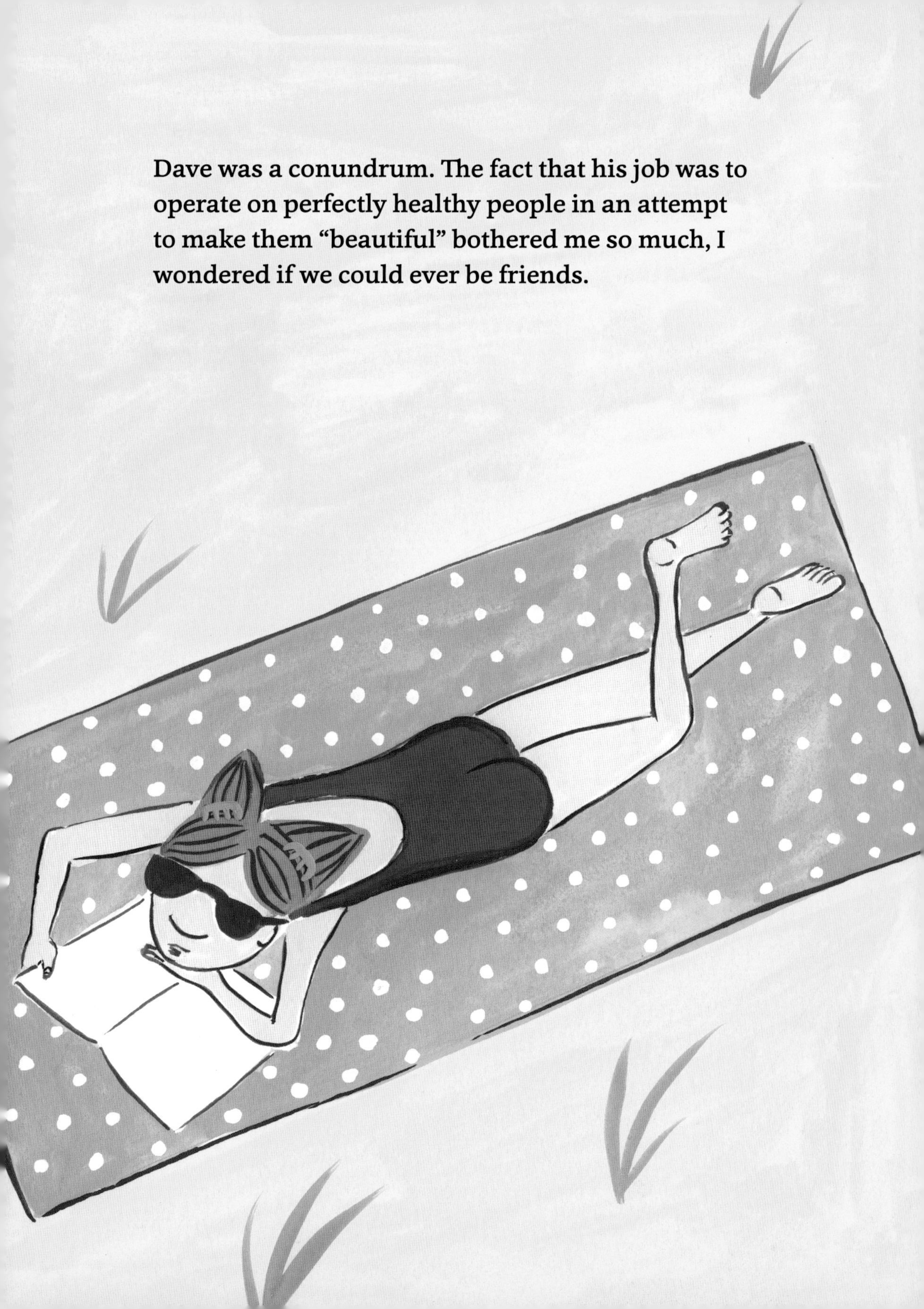

But then we spent some time together.

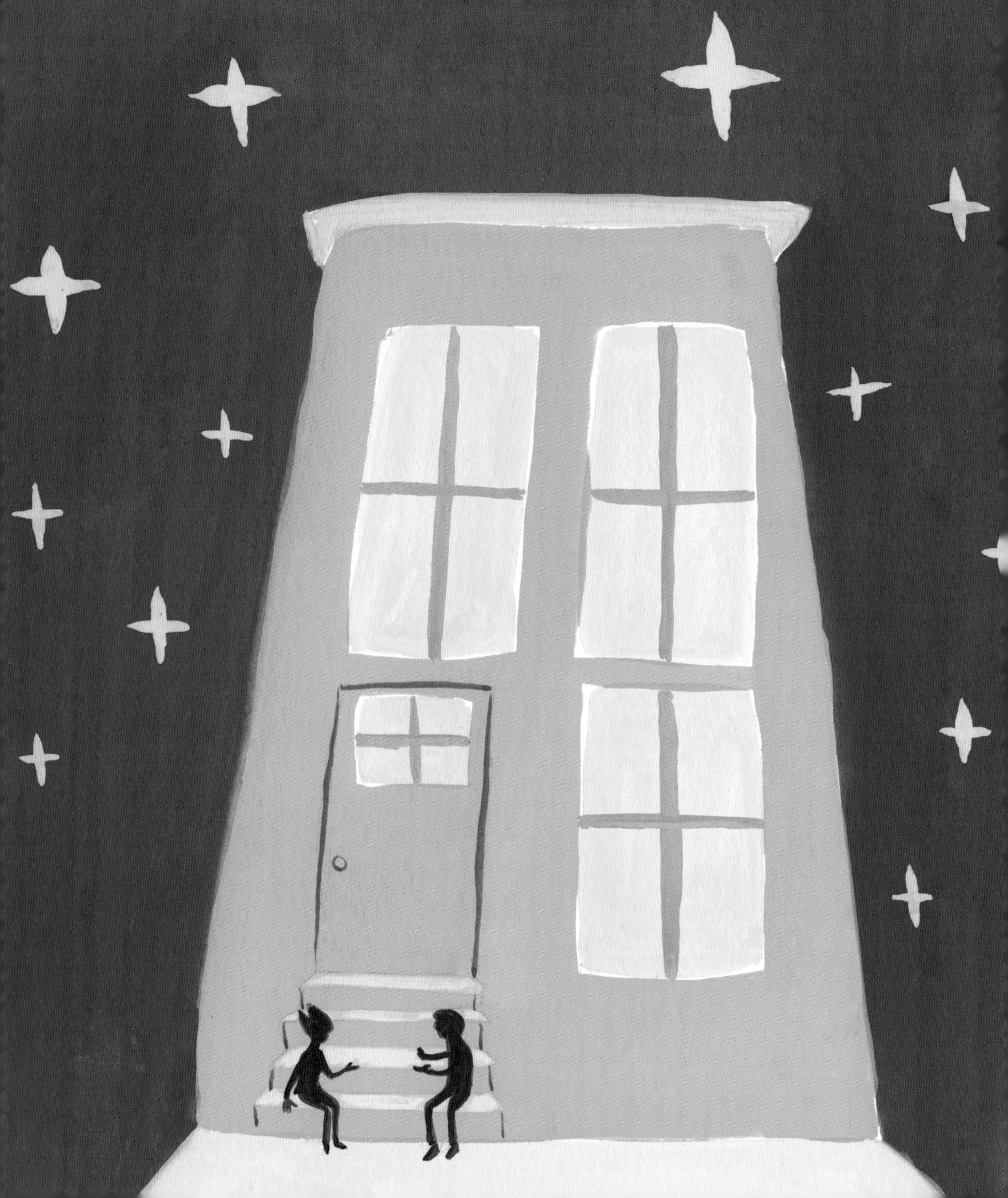

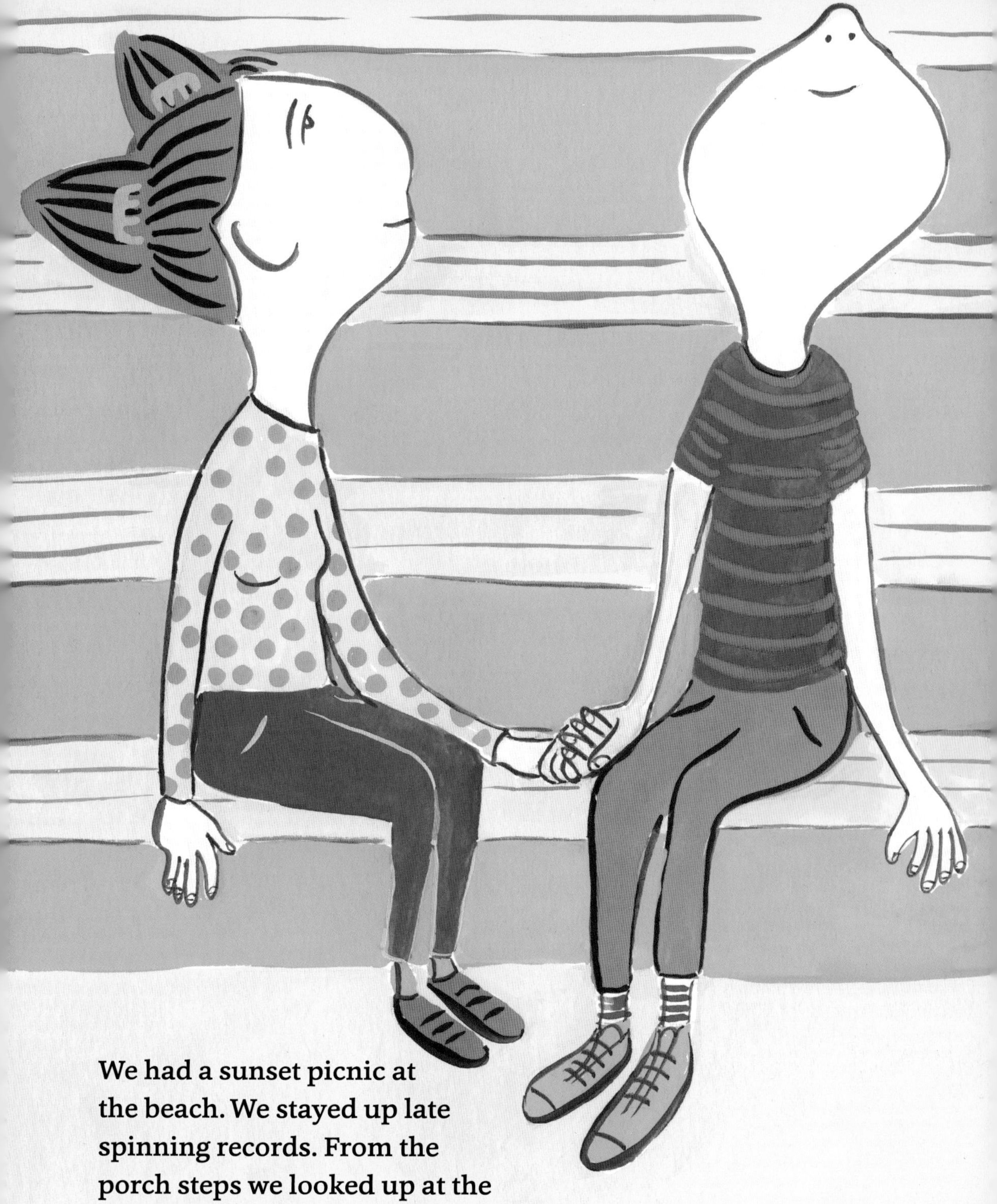

We had a sunset picnic at
the beach. We stayed up late
spinning records. From the
porch steps we looked up at the
stars, talking about everything under
them, each refusing to be the first to say goodnight.

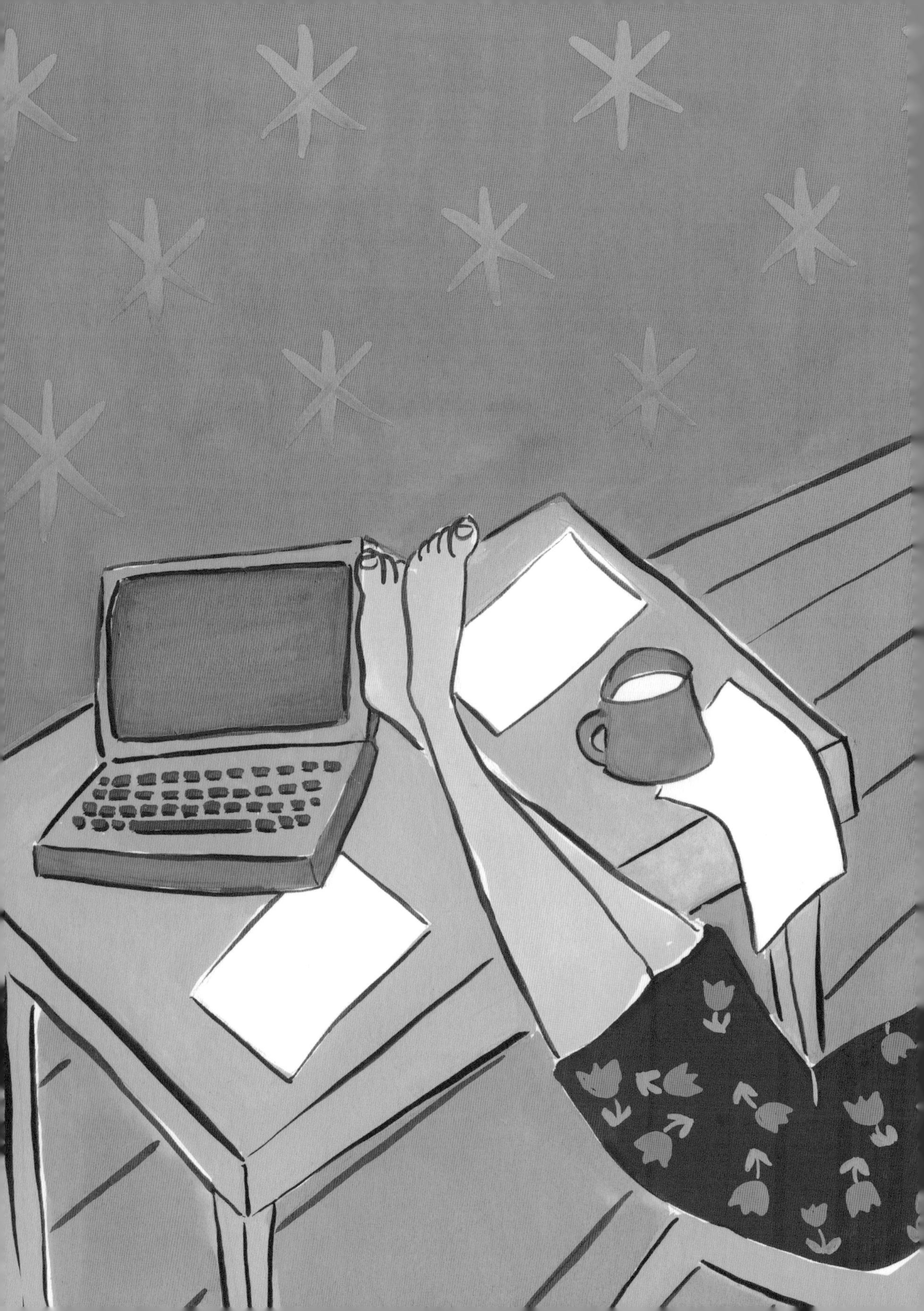

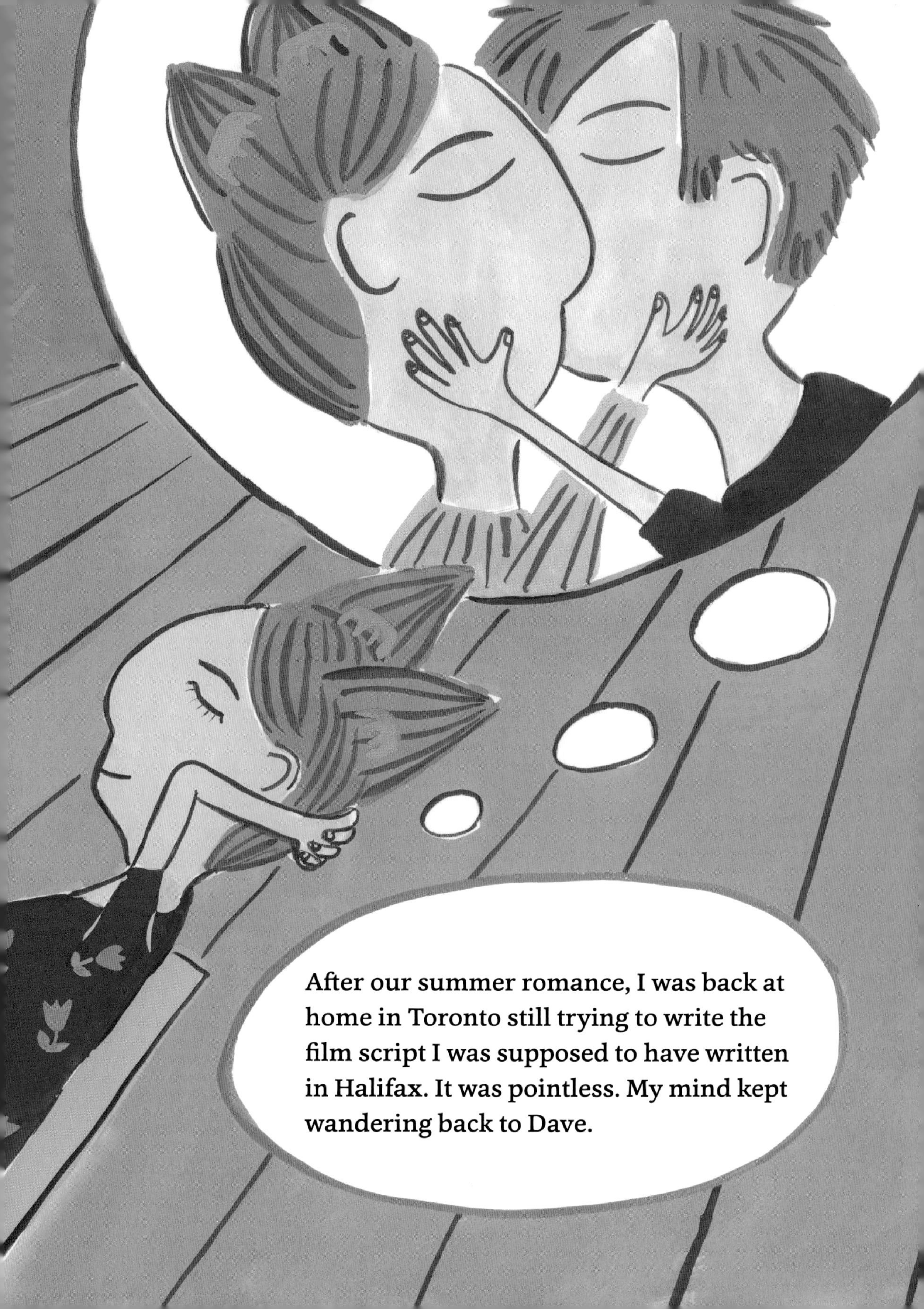
After our summer romance, I was back at home in Toronto still trying to write the film script I was supposed to have written in Halifax. It was pointless. My mind kept wandering back to Dave.

We talked about trying a long-distance relationship, but I was having second thoughts about whether or not it could work.

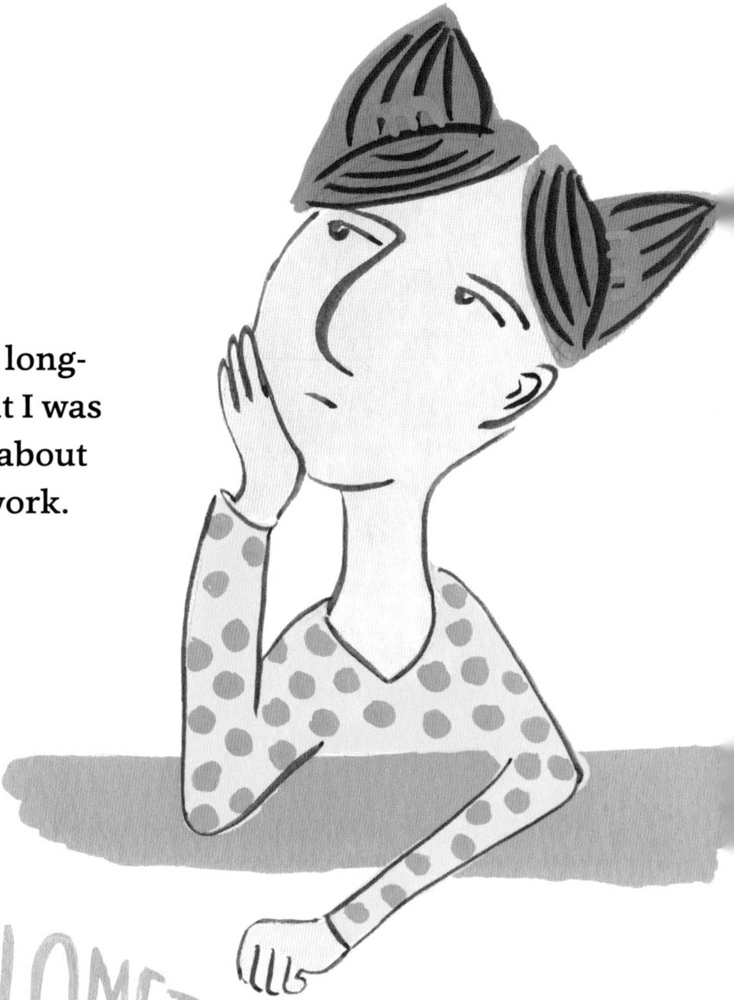

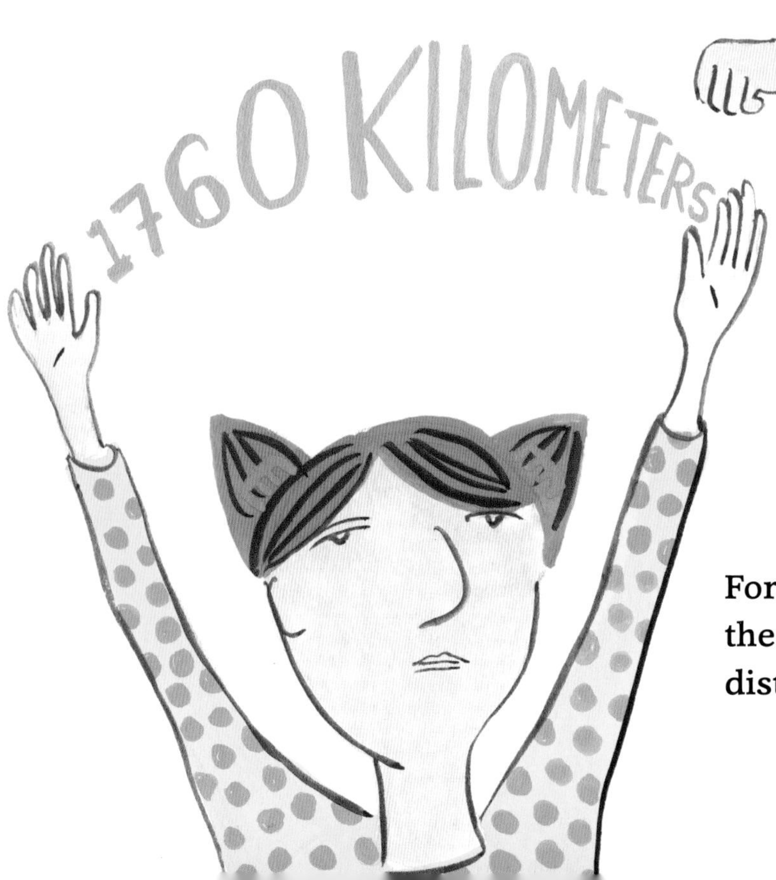
1760 KILOMETERS

For one, there was the huge and obvious distance between us.

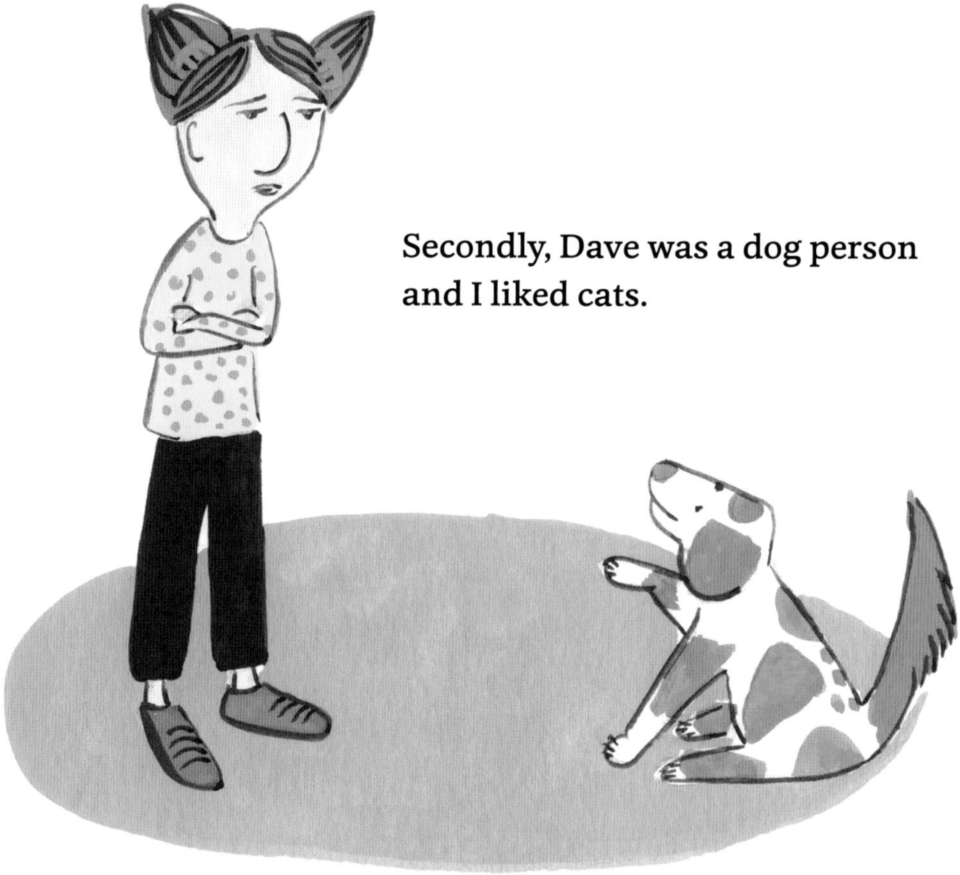

Secondly, Dave was a dog person and I liked cats.

And, finally, I'm an artist and he's a surgeon.

We were just too different.

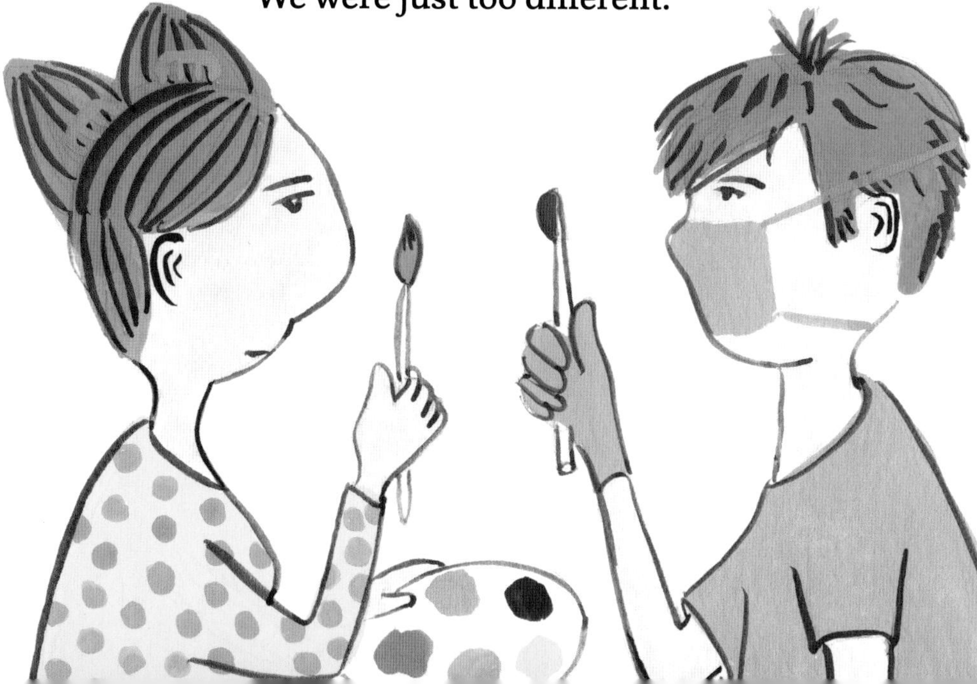

I came up with an idea to prove my point and called Dave.

“Let’s send handmade postcards to each other. It can be a collaborative art project, something to keep the conversation going.”

I waited to hear him say he thought it was a silly idea.

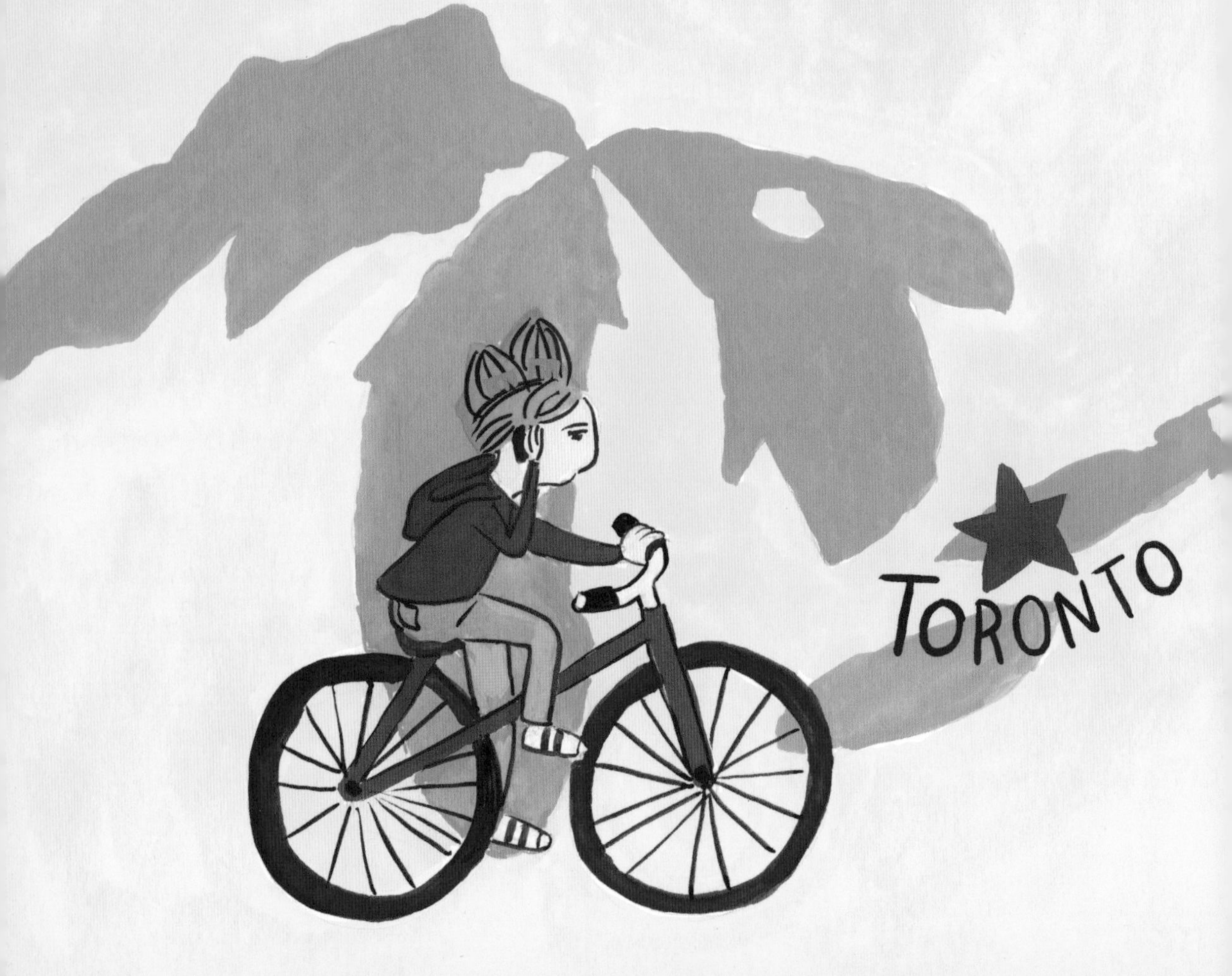
TORONTO

I could tell Dave was smiling into the phone as he said, "Sure, I'd love to."

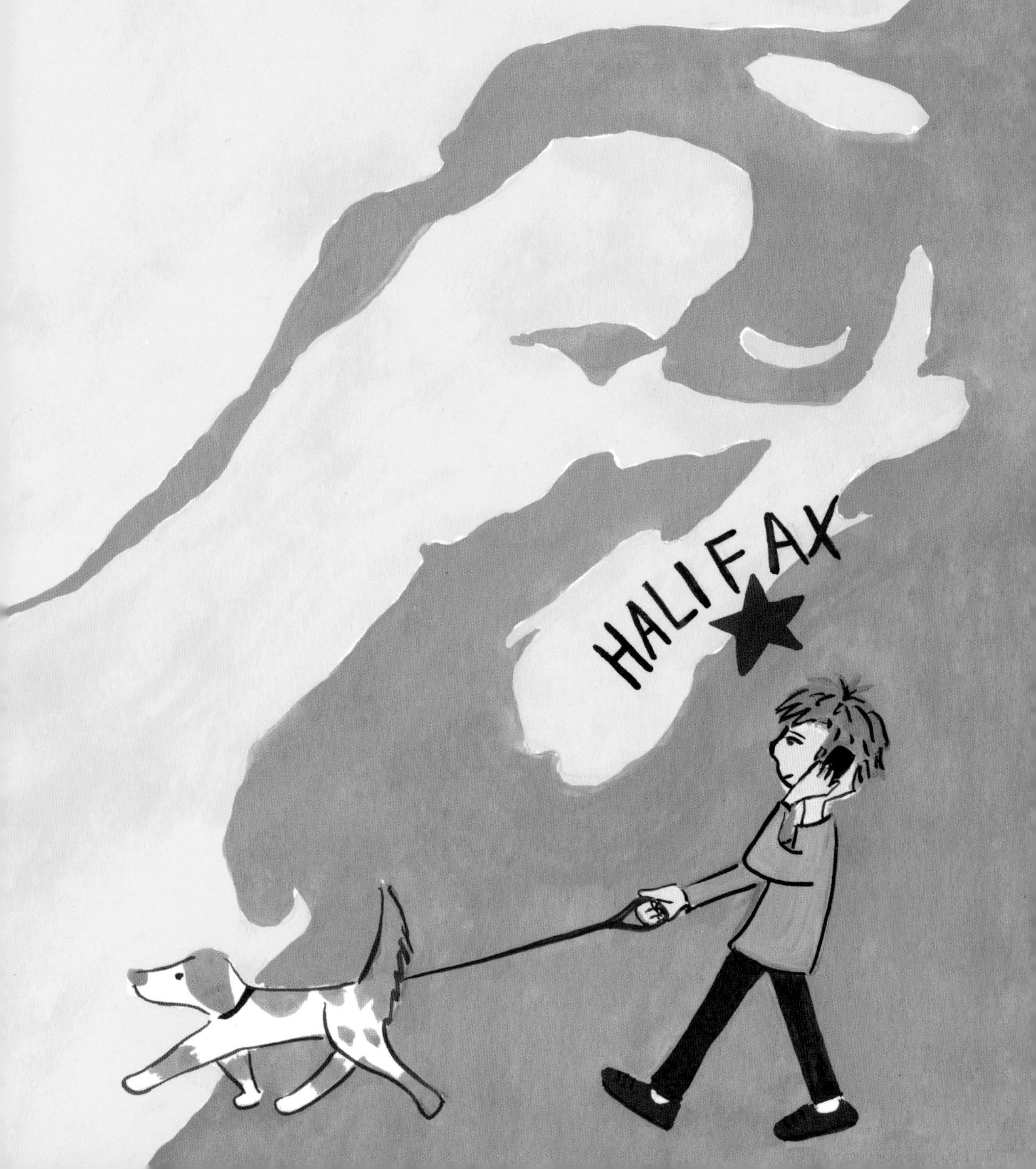
HALIFAX

The next day, I didn't even bother with my film.
Instead, I made a postcard for Dave.

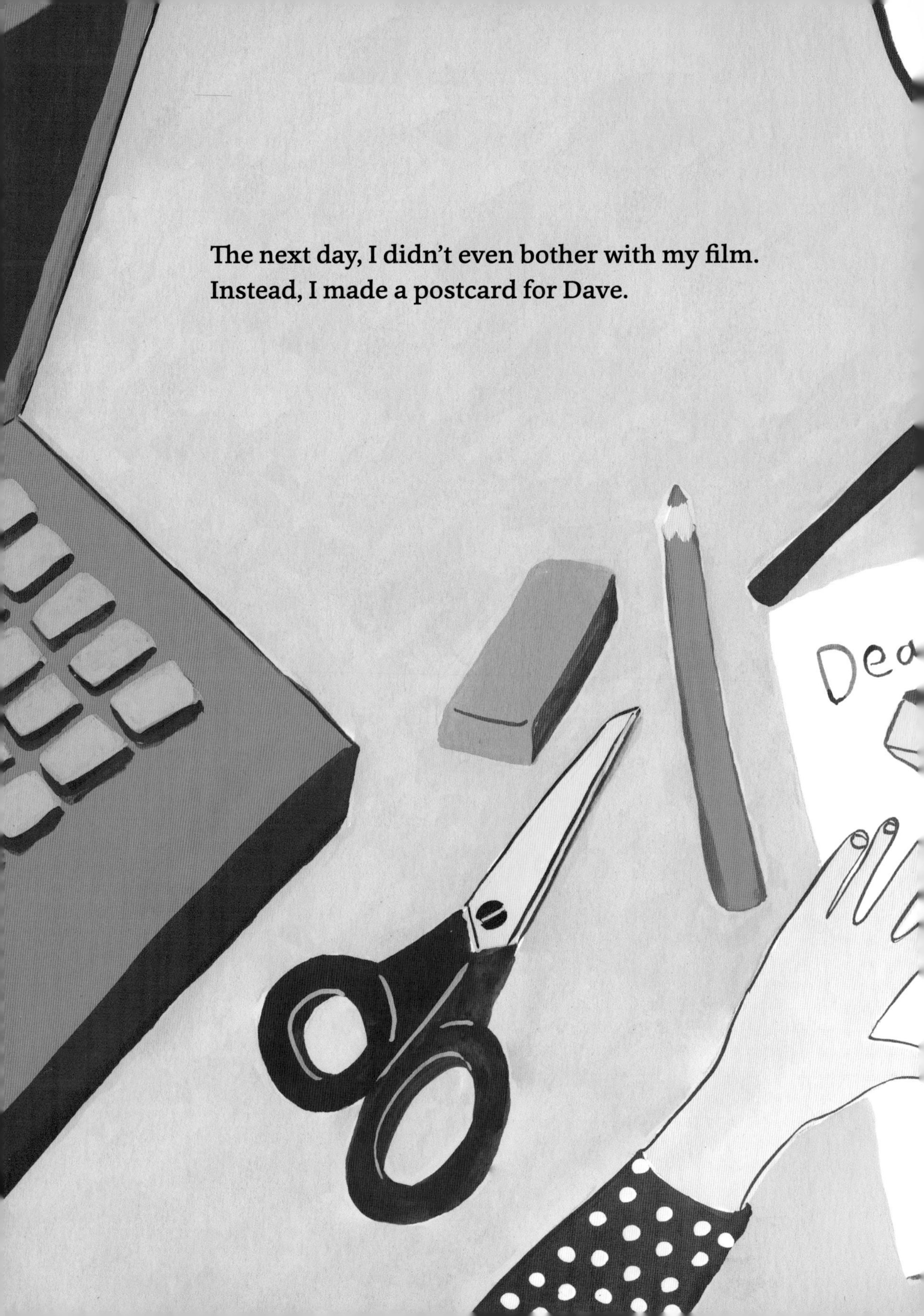
Dea

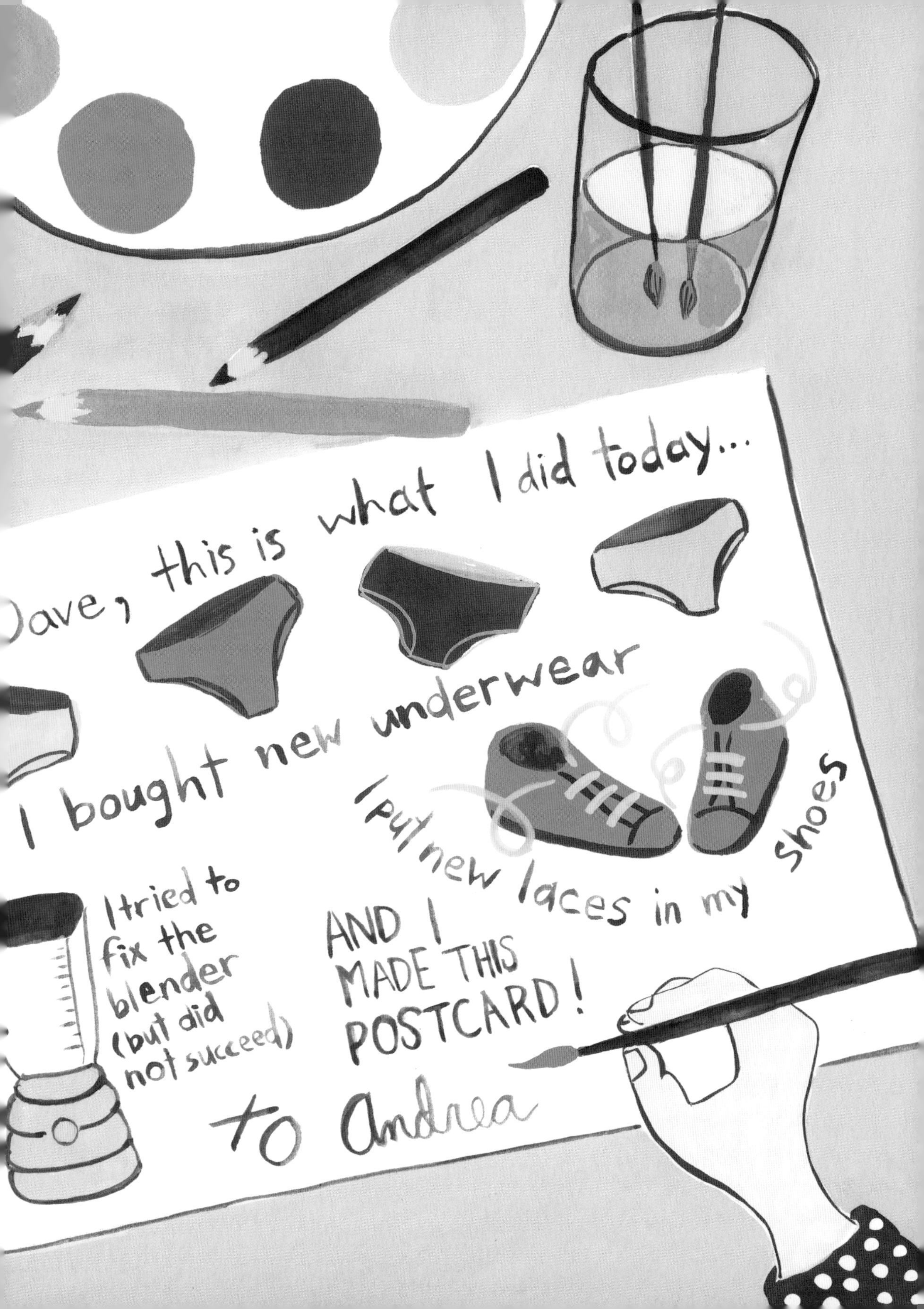

Dave, this is what I did today...
I bought new underwear
I put new laces in my shoes
I tried to fix the blender (but did not succeed)
AND I MADE THIS POSTCARD!
to Andrea

A few days later I received Dave's postcard in the mail. It showed how on that day he had removed skin cancer from different parts of different patients' bodies and then grafted, patched and sewed their skin up again.

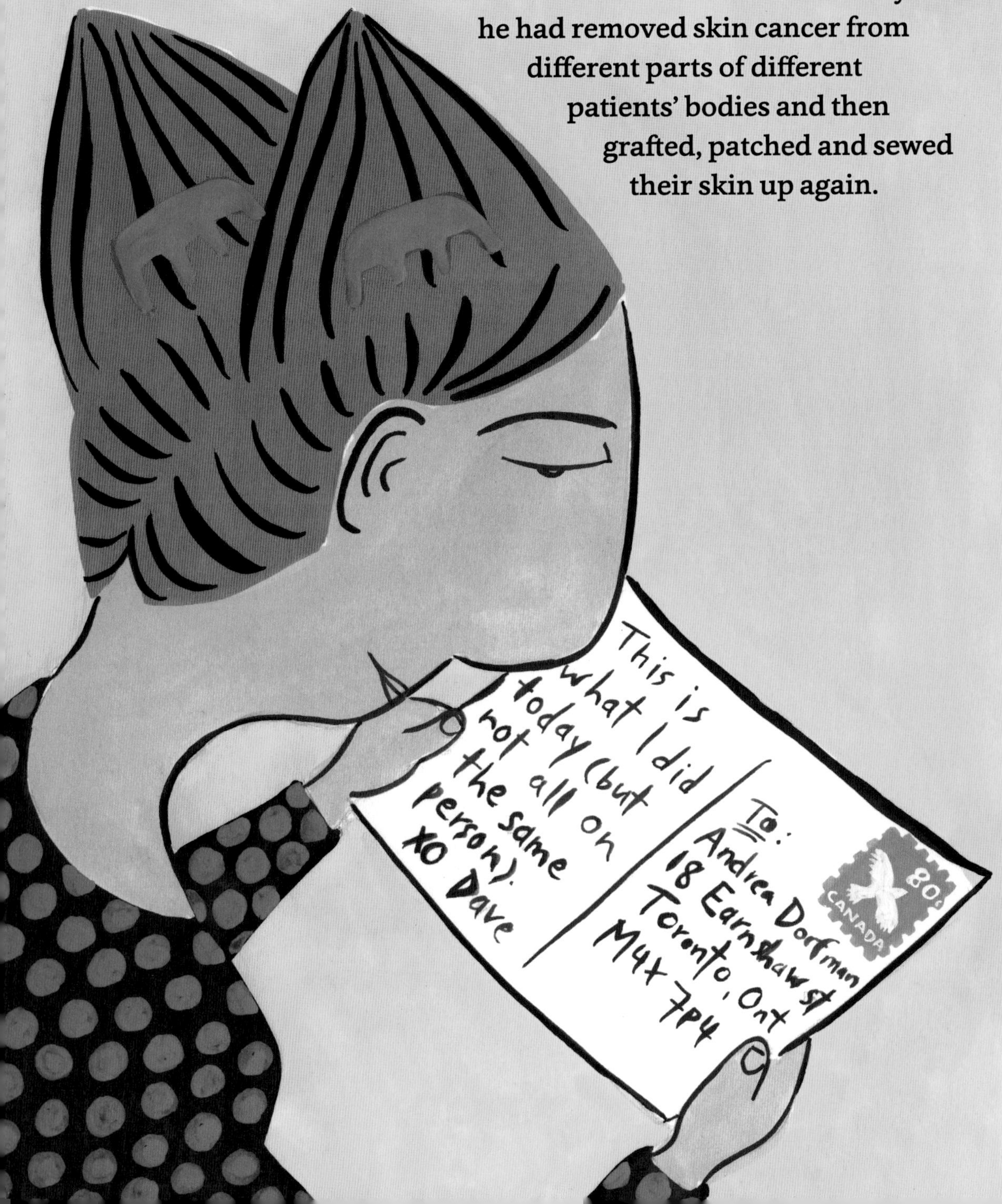

This is what I did today (but not all on the same person).
XO Dave
To:
Andrea Dorfman
18 Earnshaw St
Toronto, Ont
M4x 7P4
80¢
CANADA

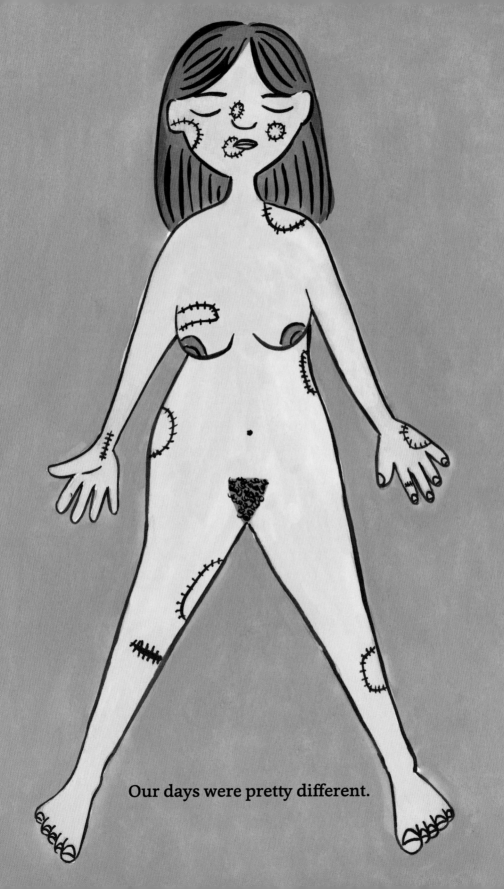

Our days were pretty different.

Many weeks (and postcards) later, I visited Dave in Halifax. We were walking his dog, Roxy, when he received an emergency call to go to the hospital.

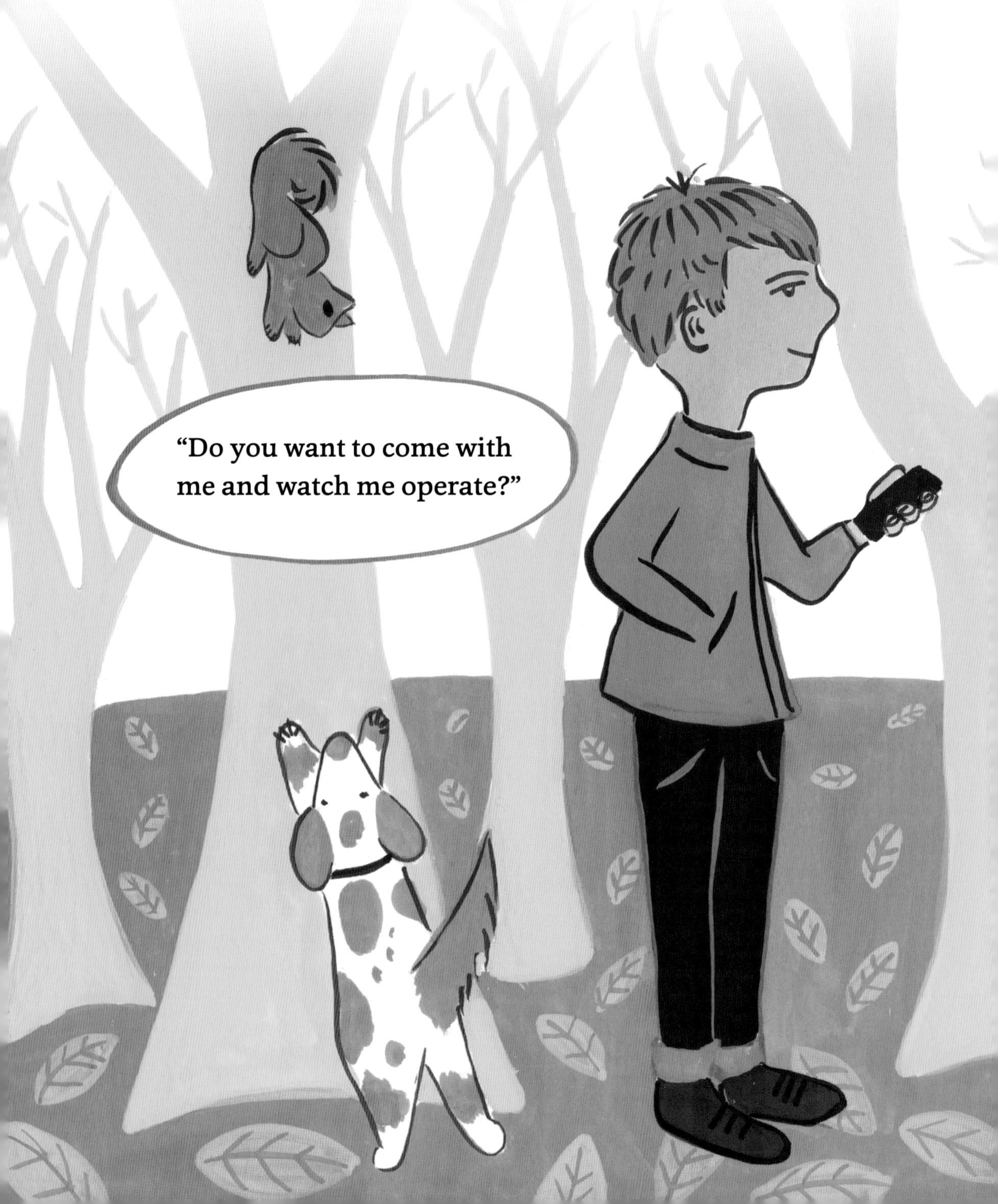
"Do you want to come with me and watch me operate?"

I'd never seen an operation before and I was a little nervous about the blood. What if I passed out? I took a deep breath.

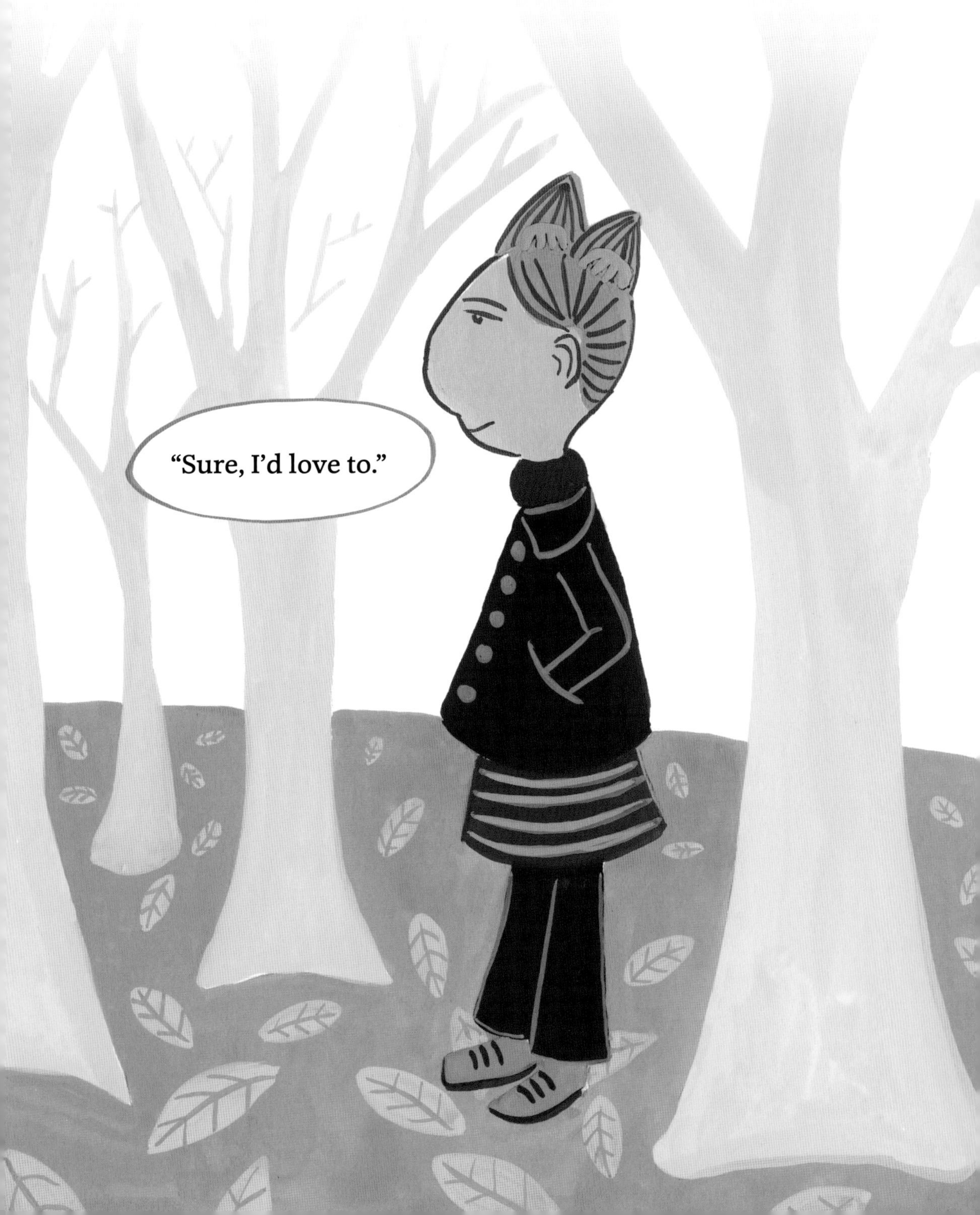
"Sure, I'd love to."

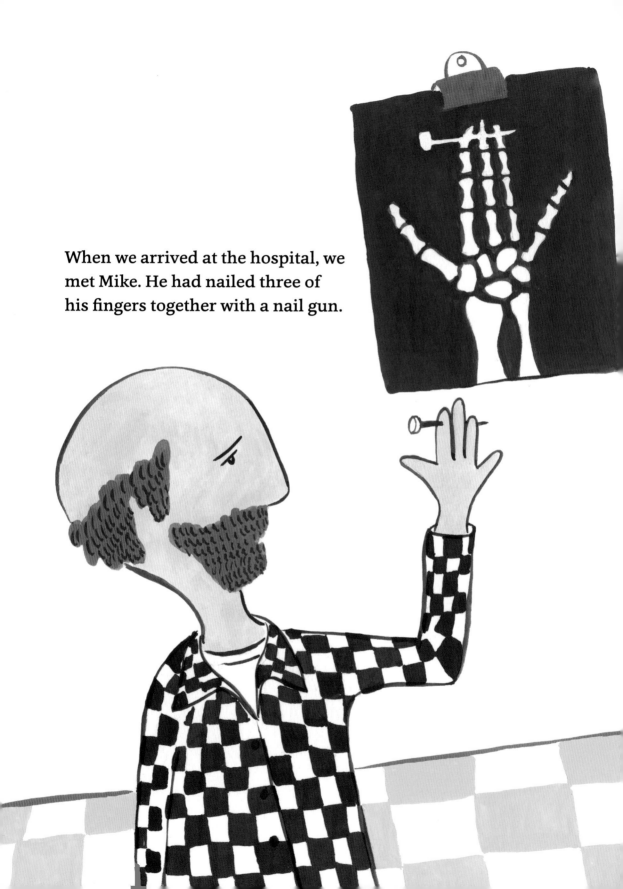

When we arrived at the hospital, we met Mike. He had nailed three of his fingers together with a nail gun.

Dave froze Mike's hand. He then carefully removed the nail and fixed up each of Mike's fingers, one by one. I was so enthralled watching Dave operate that I forgot to pass out. At the end of the operation, Mike's hand looked as good as new. (Well, swollen and red, but you know what I mean.) I understood then that Dave was truly an artist!

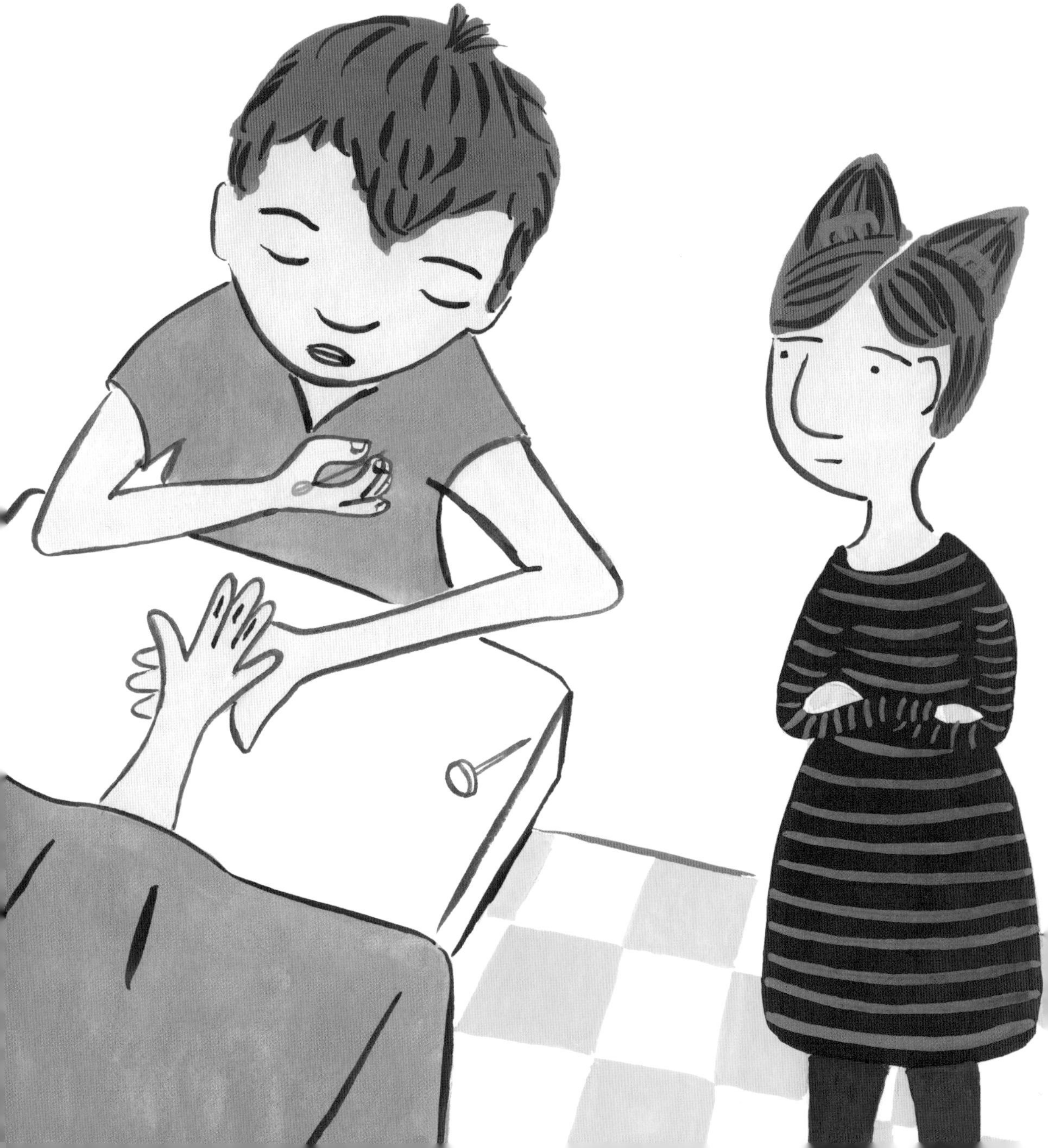

I was beginning to appreciate all the ways that Dave could help people through plastic surgery. But the night before I flew home he told me something that troubled me as much as his artistry in fixing Mike's hand had impressed me.

"A mother brought in her eight-year-old son today because his ears stuck out," he said.

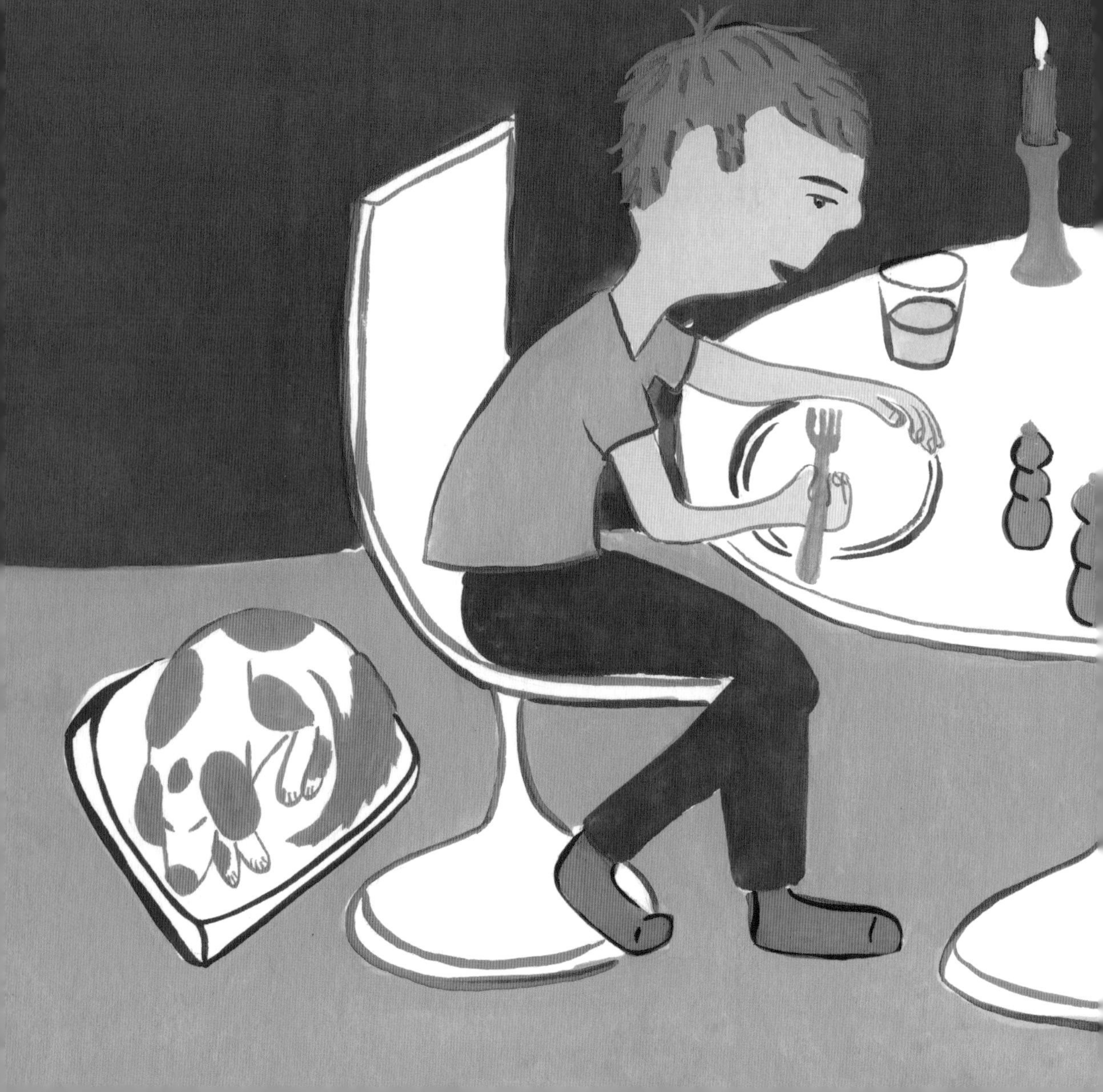

"Are sticking-out-ears a problem?" I asked.

"She was worried he'd be made fun of so she wanted me to operate," he replied.

"You're not going to do it, are you?"

"Yeah, I did it today."

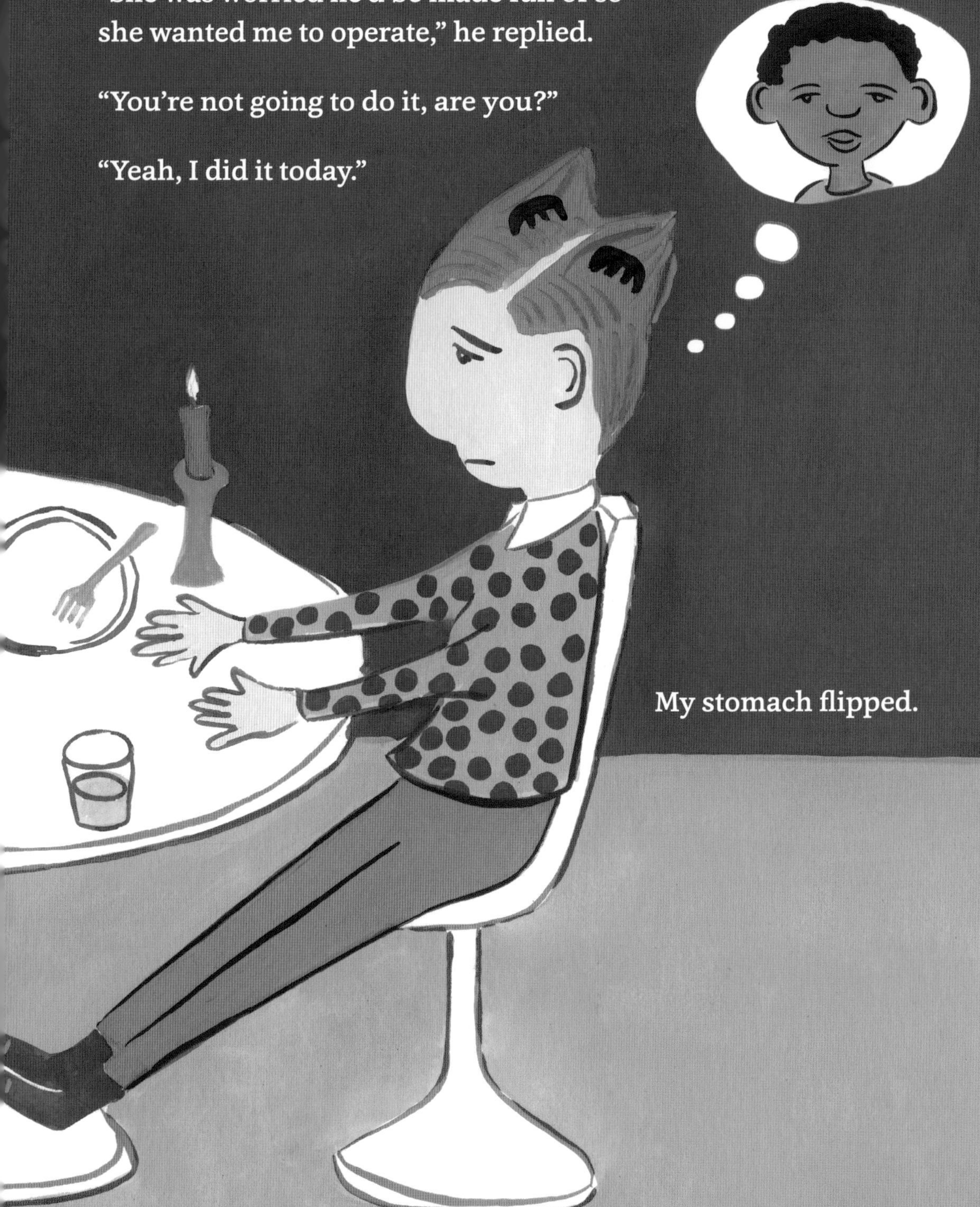

My stomach flipped.

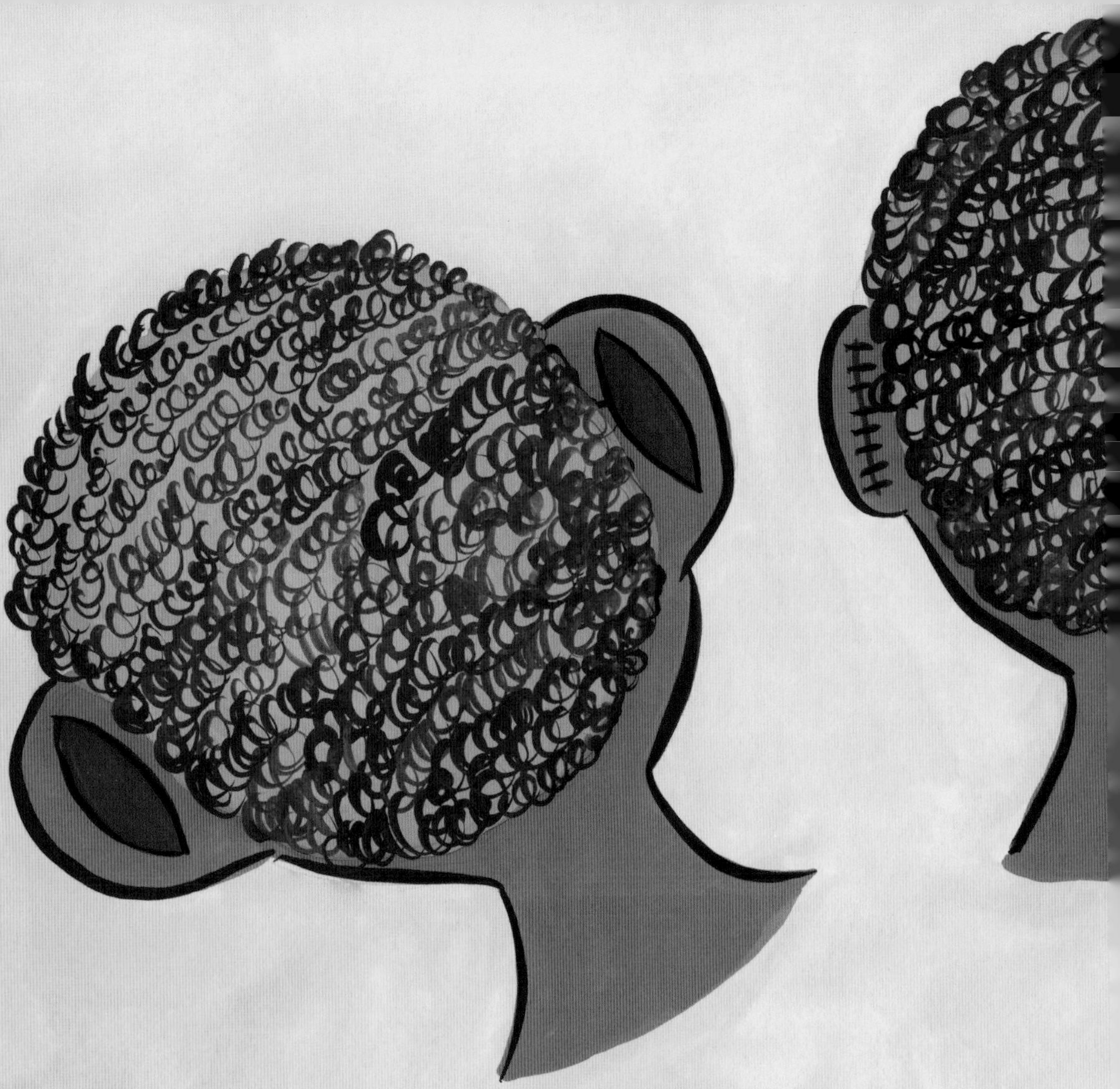

Dave described the procedure to me. An incision was made in the crease behind each of the boy's ears and then the cartilage was reshaped. Afterward, it was sewn with non-removable stitches to the sides of the boy's skull where his ears would heal much flatter against his head.

Dave's voice faded out. I couldn't believe he did an operation on a perfectly healthy little boy just because the kid's mom thought he'd get made fun of.

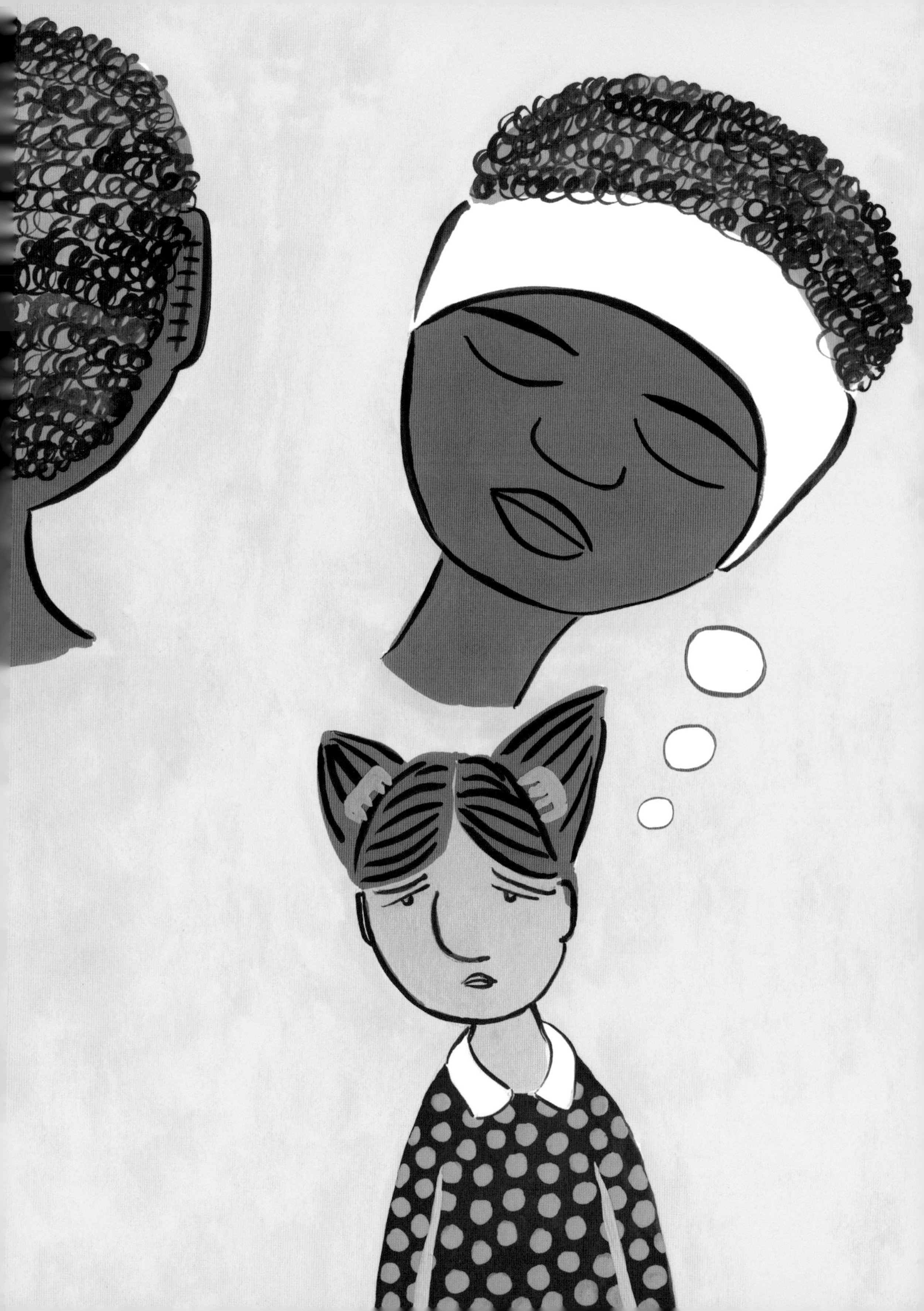

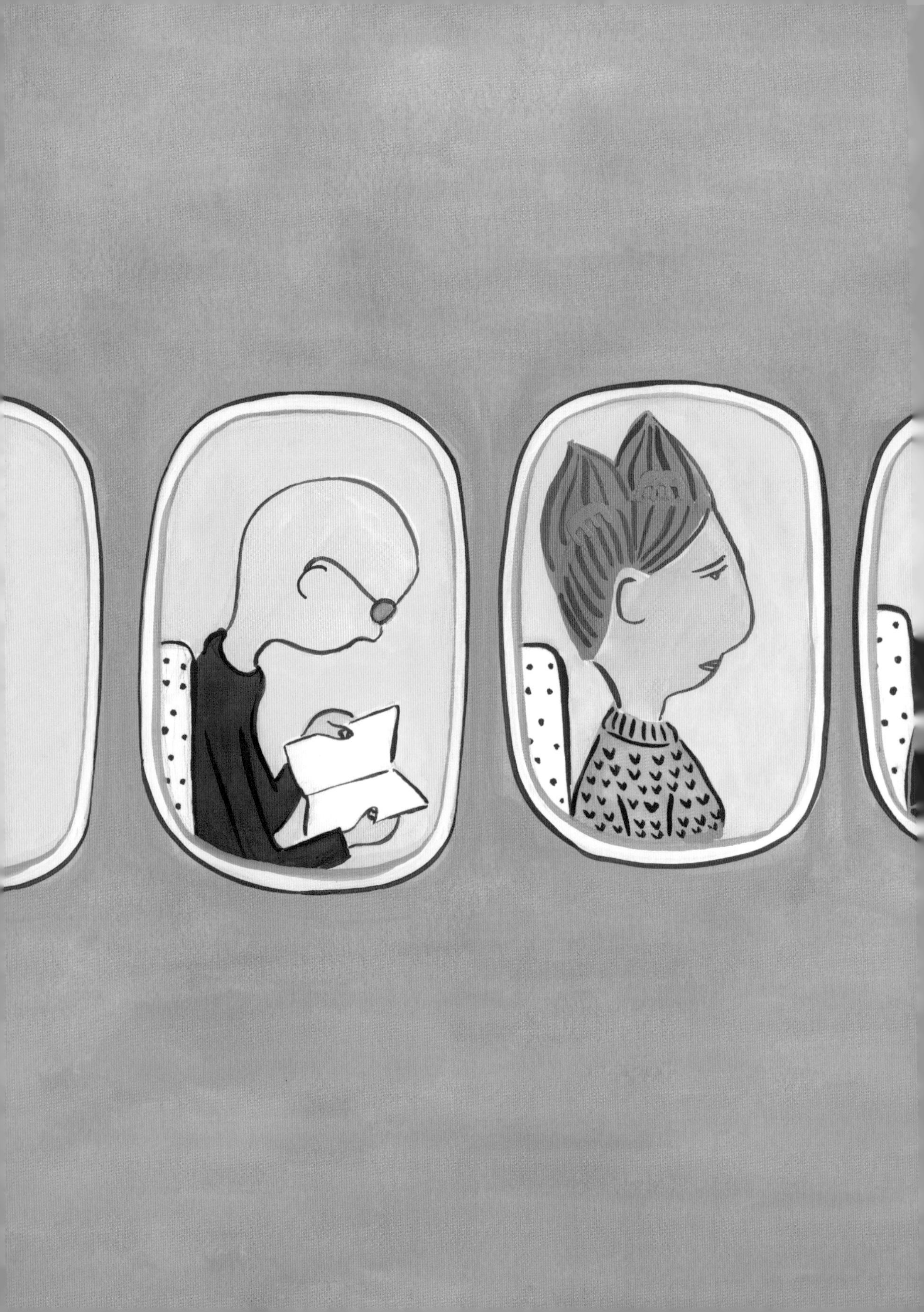

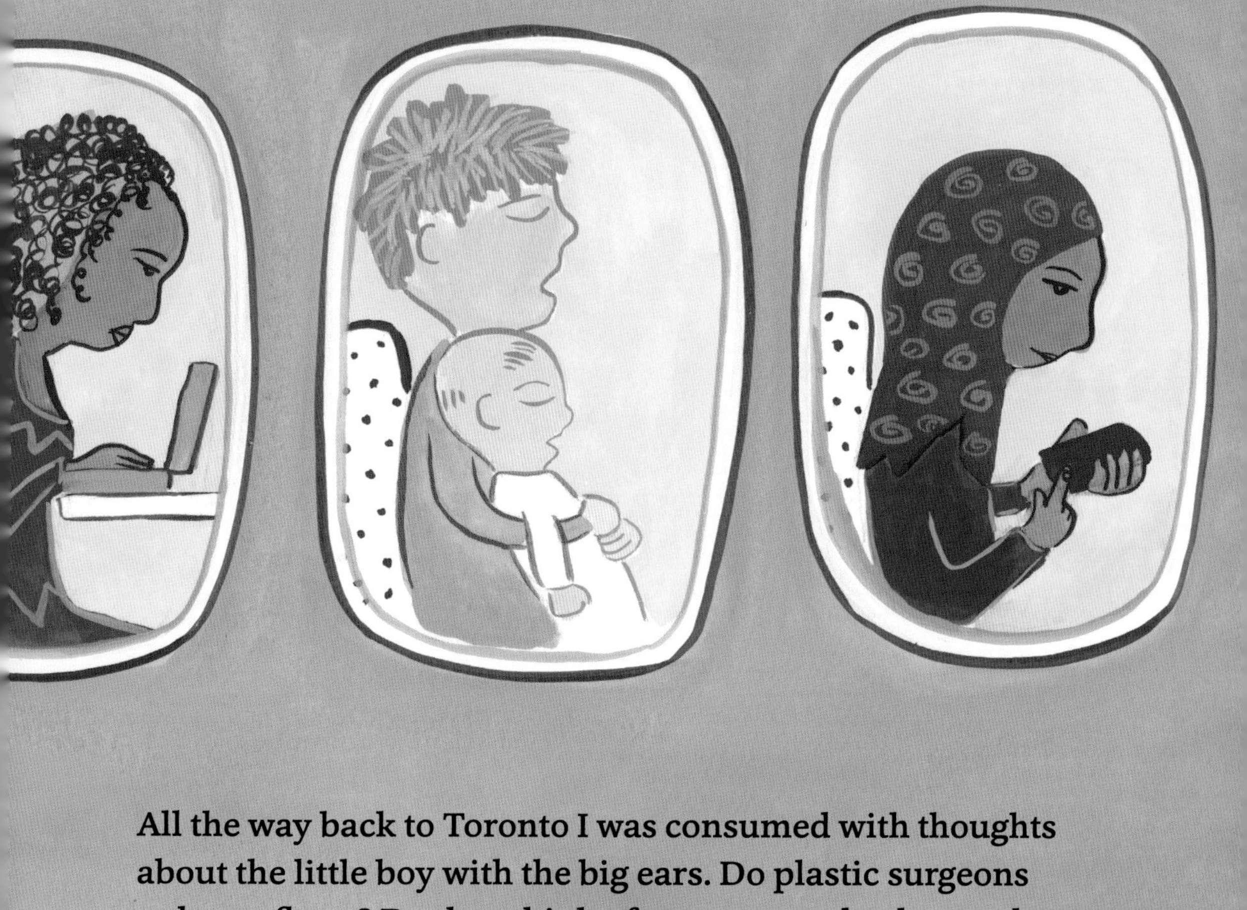

All the way back to Toronto I was consumed with thoughts about the little boy with the big ears. Do plastic surgeons only see flaws? Do they think of everyone as broken and in need of repair? Do they think they hold the key to beauty? The more I thought about these questions, the more I thought about my childhood.

Grade 2

When I was a little kid, I wasn't a pretty girl — but I was pretty cute. My hair was fine and always tangled in a big puffball at the back of my head. I had buckteeth and a scar under my nose from a bad tobogganing accident. I didn't care about what I looked like back then. Why would I?

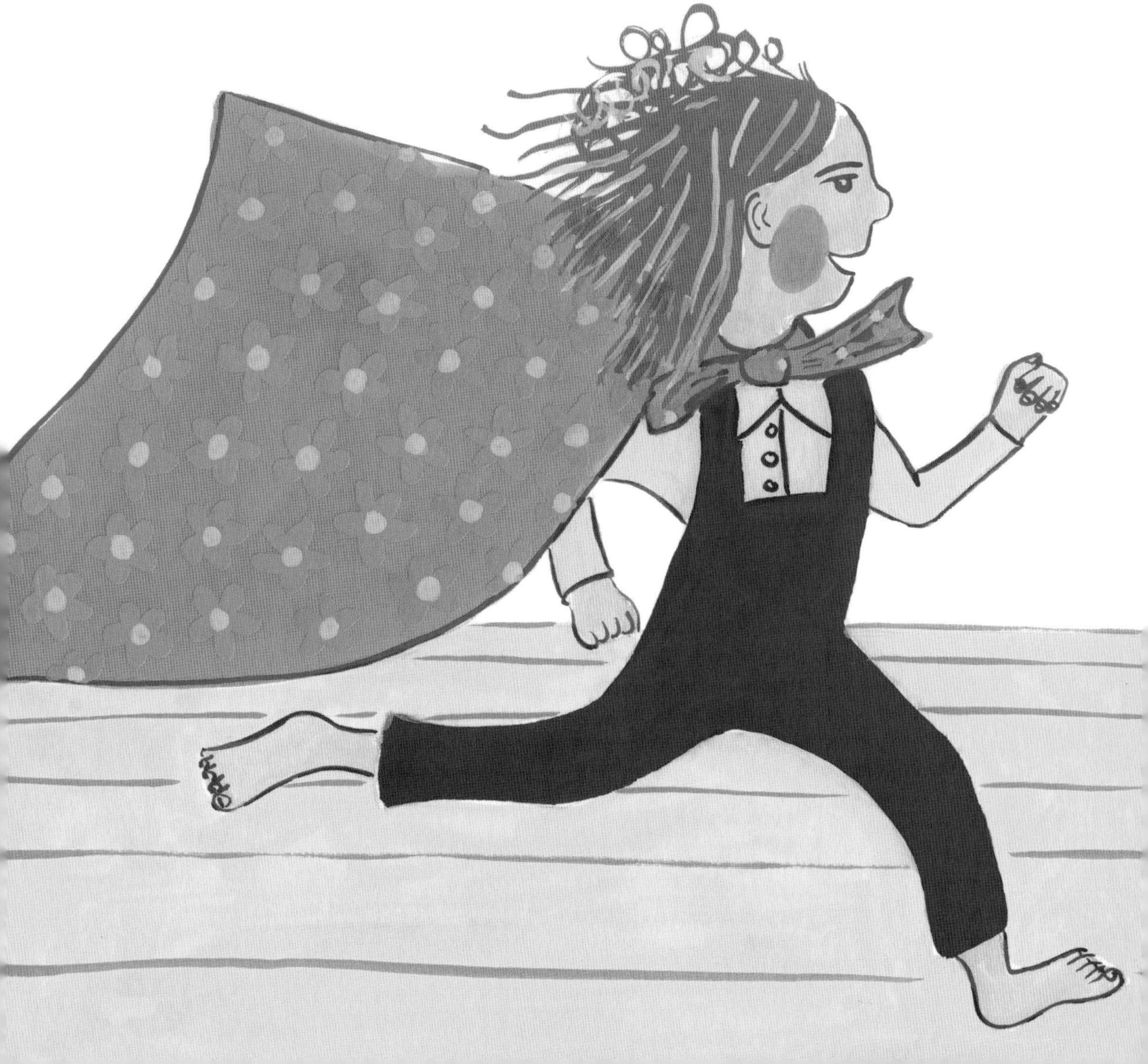

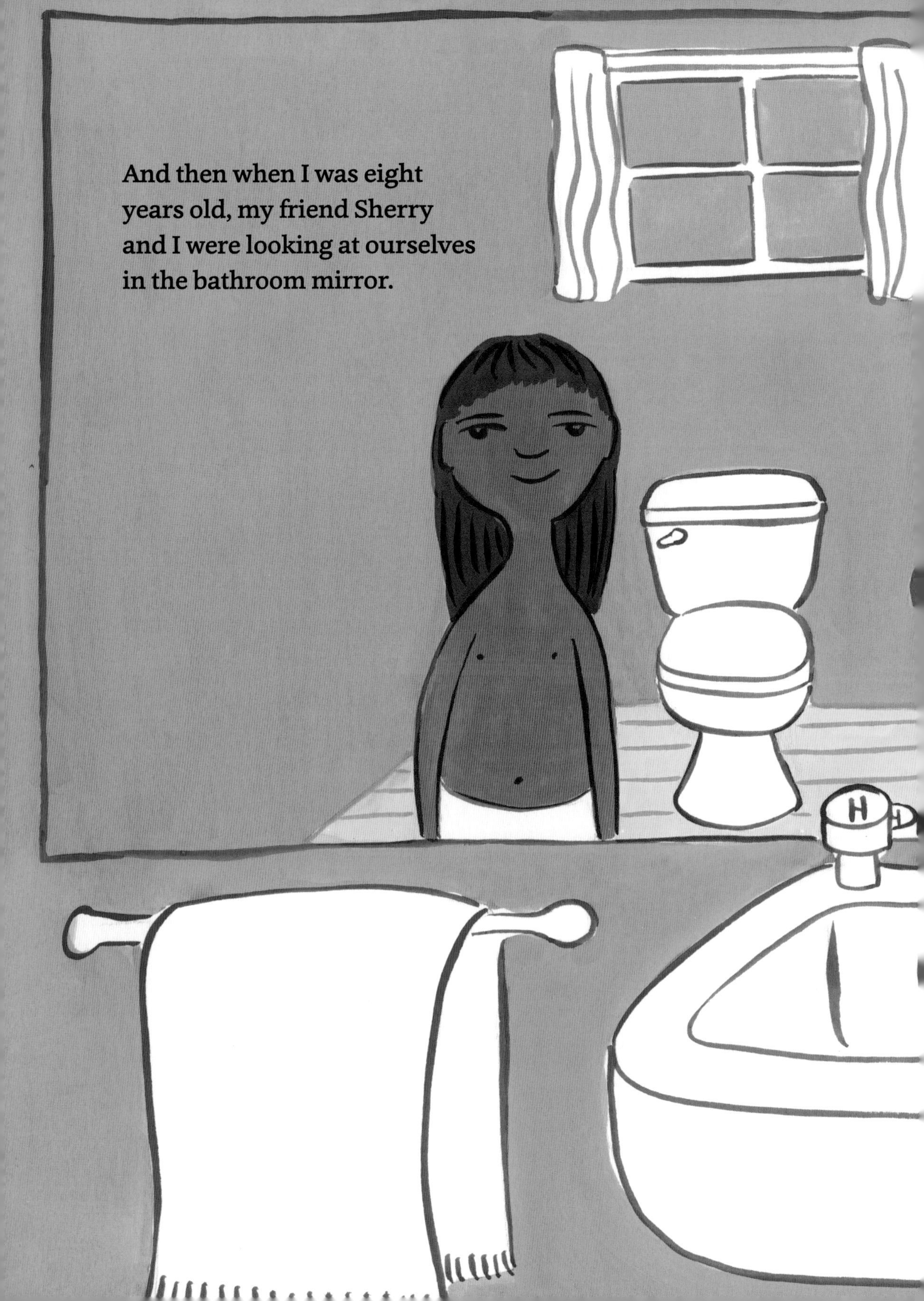
And then when I was eight
years old, my friend Sherry
and I were looking at ourselves
in the bathroom mirror.

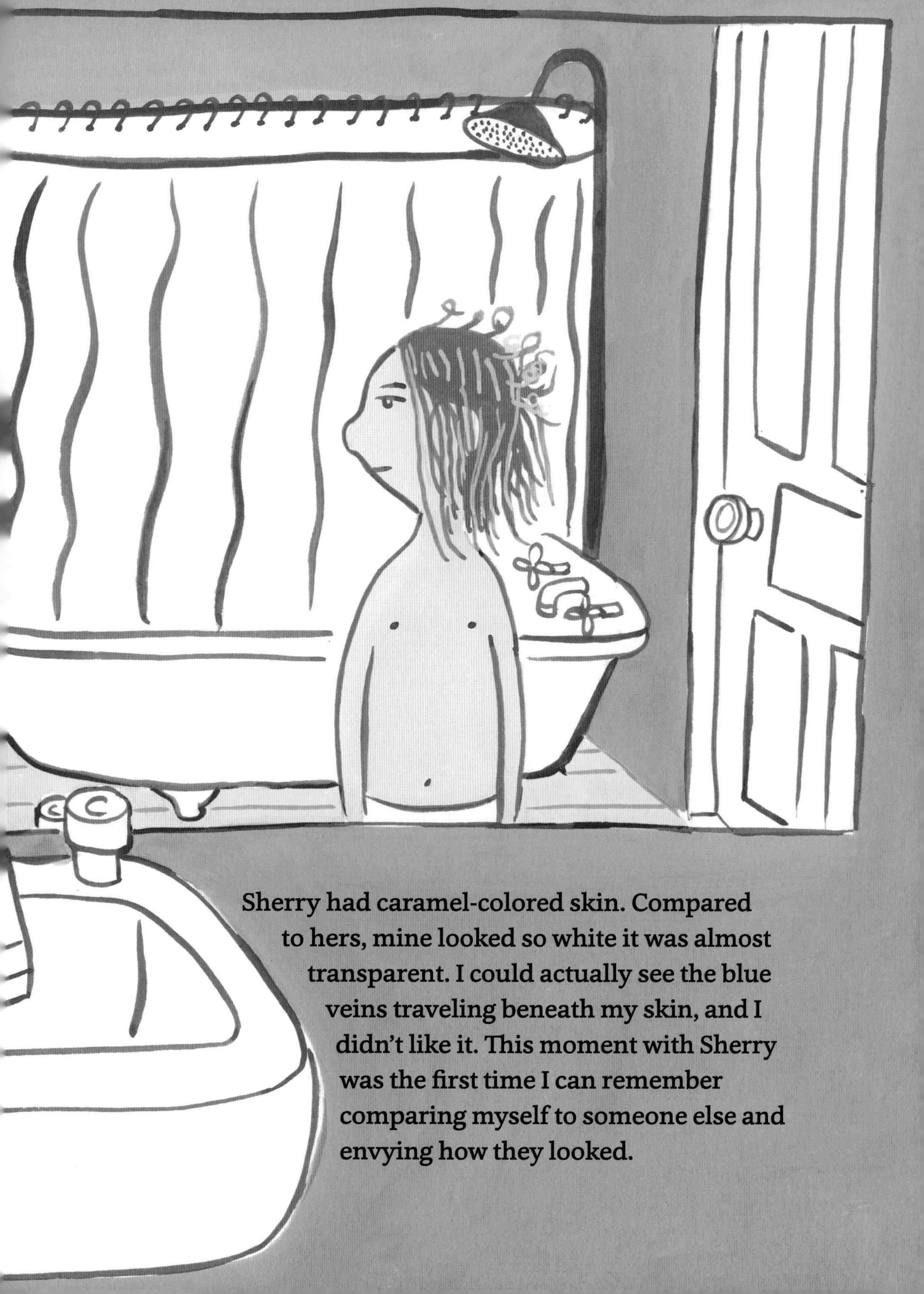

Sherry had caramel-colored skin. Compared to hers, mine looked so white it was almost transparent. I could actually see the blue veins traveling beneath my skin, and I didn't like it. This moment with Sherry was the first time I can remember comparing myself to someone else and envying how they looked.

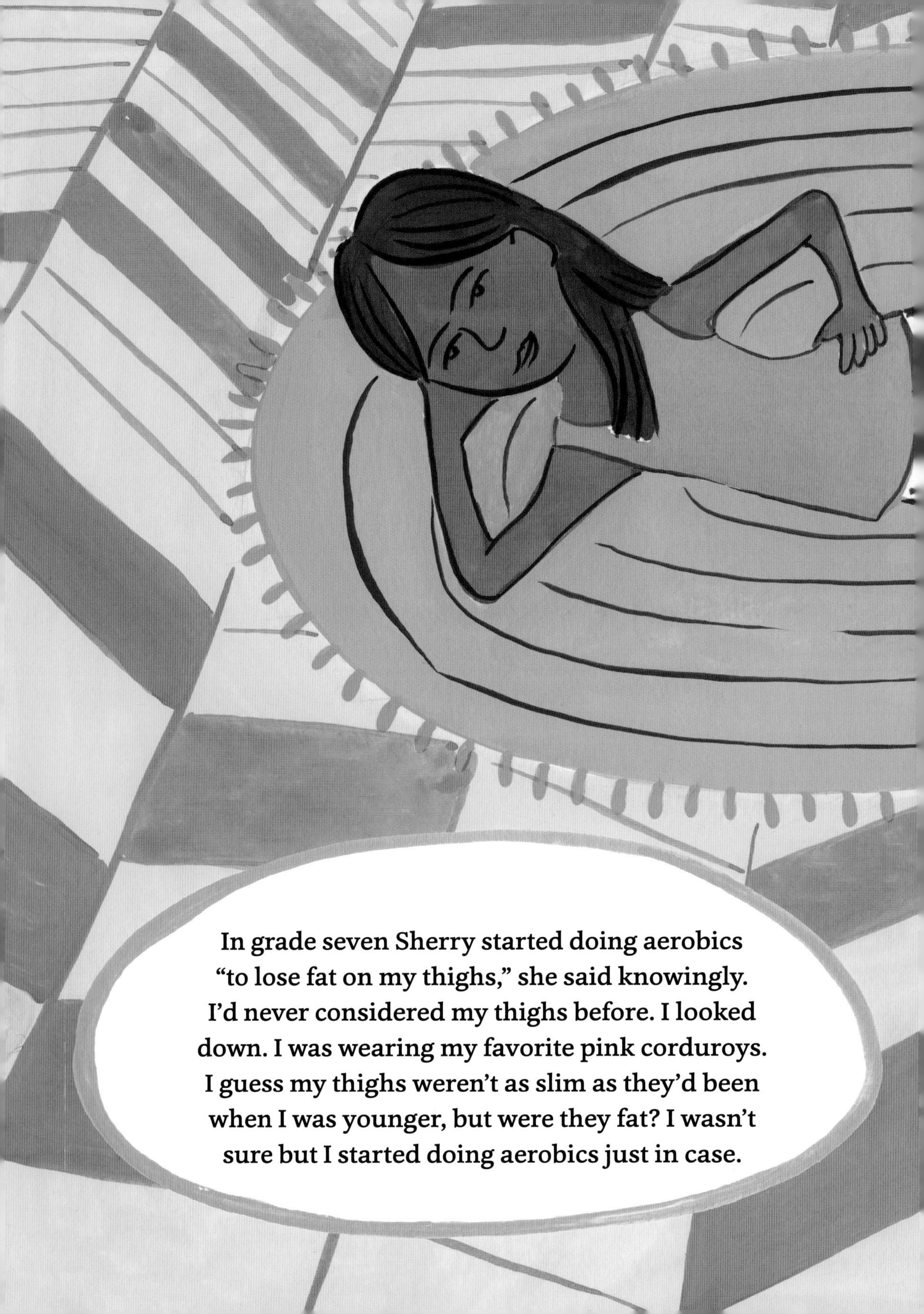

In grade seven Sherry started doing aerobics "to lose fat on my thighs," she said knowingly. I'd never considered my thighs before. I looked down. I was wearing my favorite pink corduroys. I guess my thighs weren't as slim as they'd been when I was younger, but were they fat? I wasn't sure but I started doing aerobics just in case.

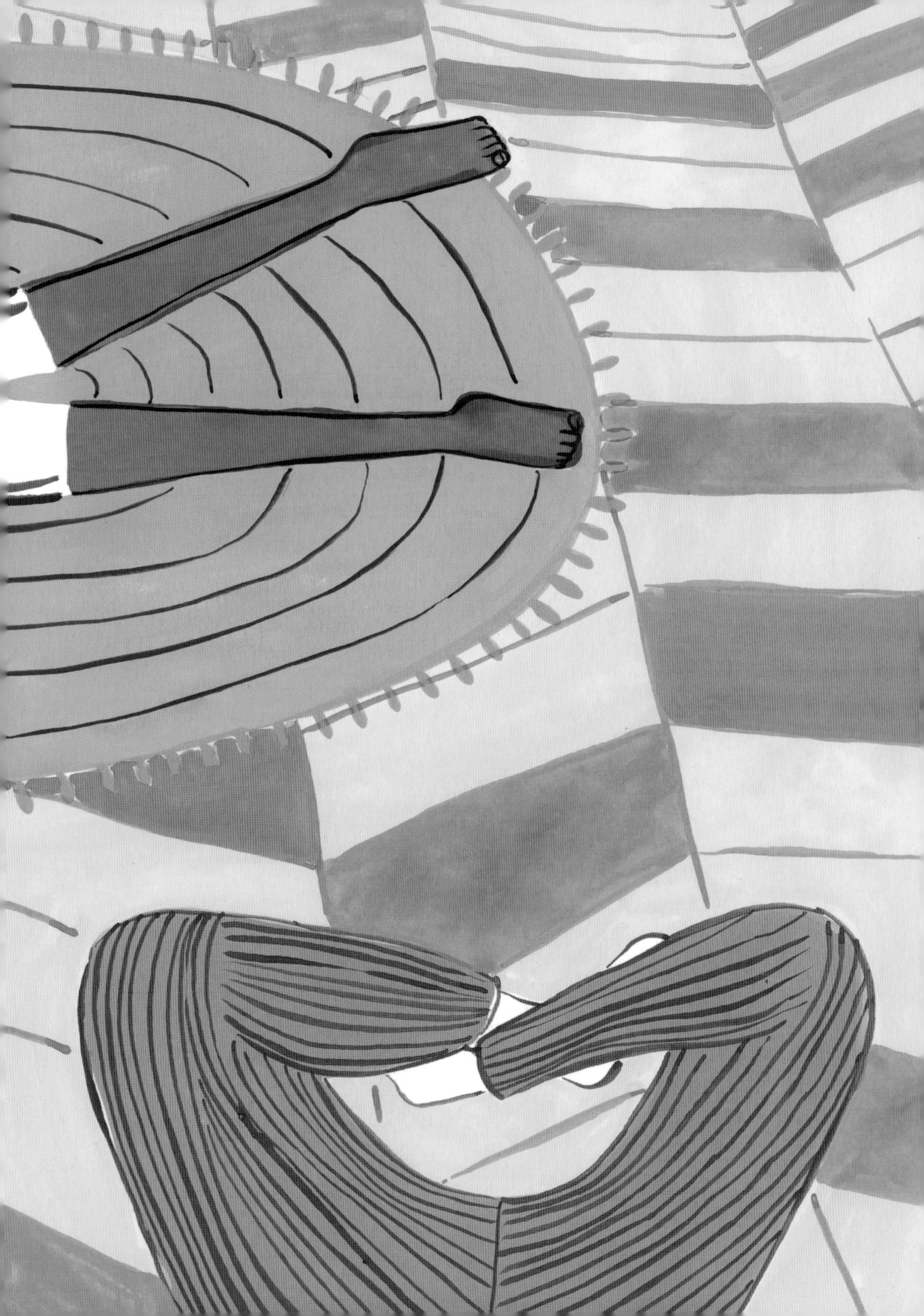

But then things really started to change. My entire body began to feel warped and off-kilter. I got pimples, breasts and my period. My fine hair became dark and oily, and I felt self-conscious and strange.

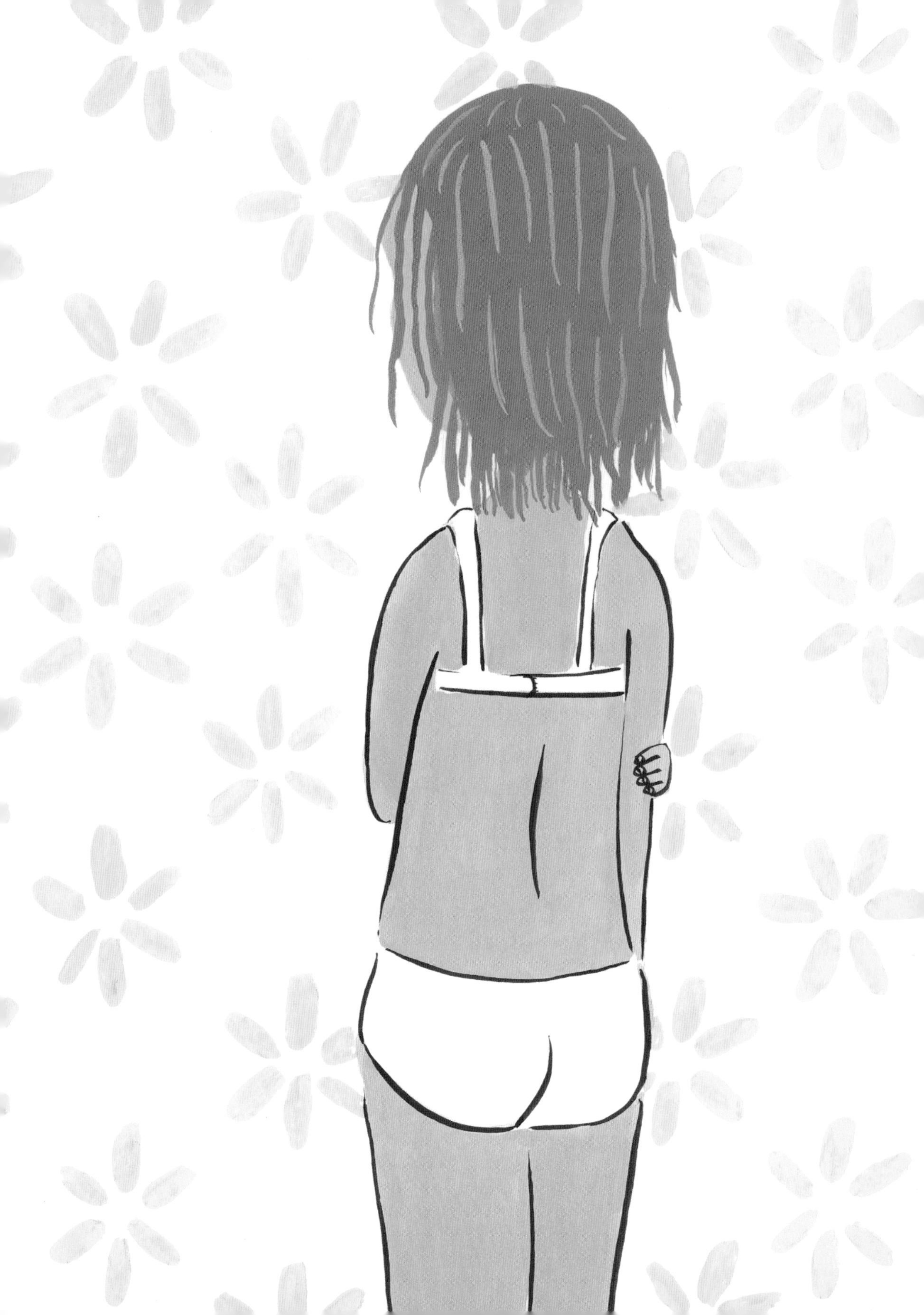

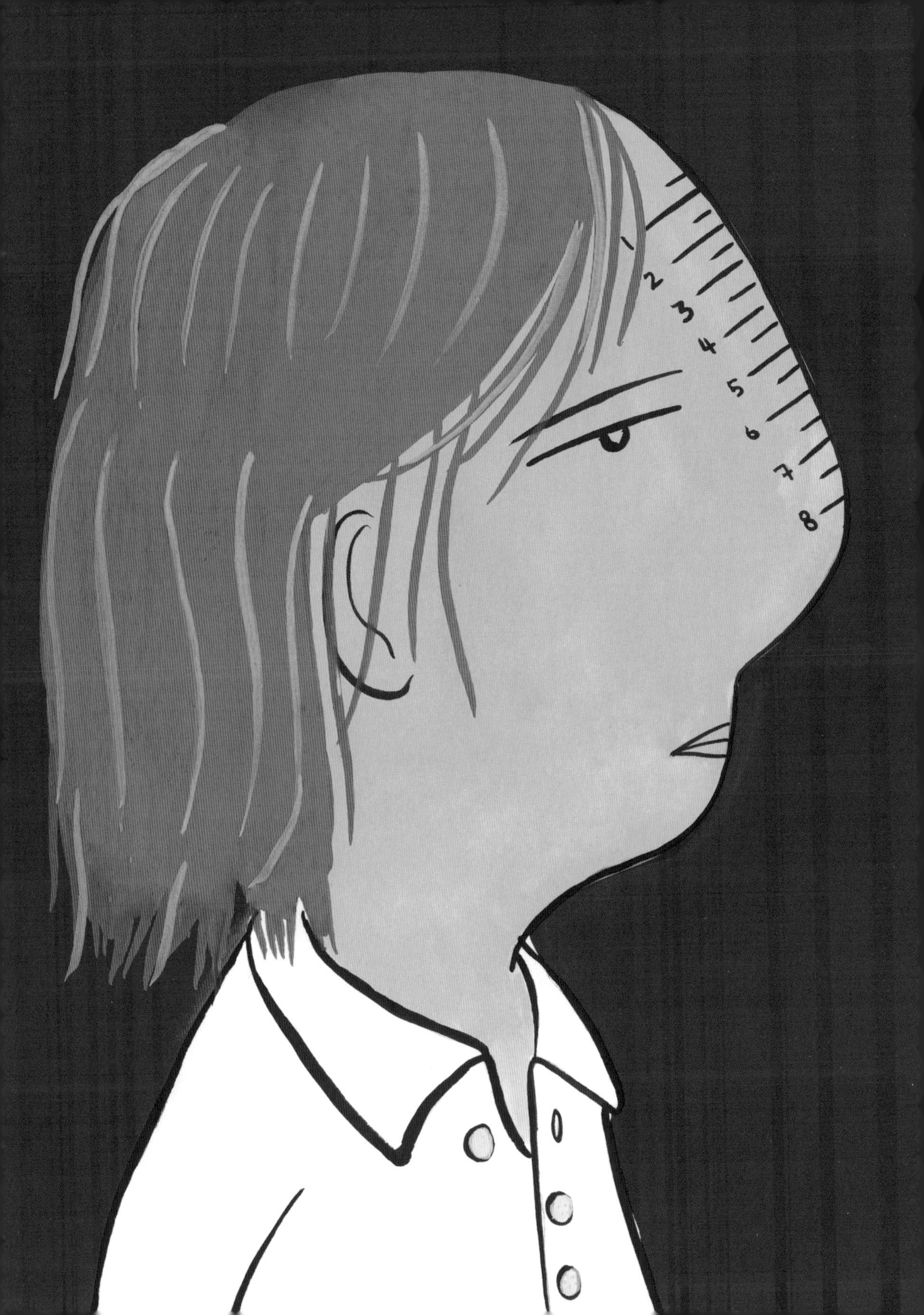
1
2
3
4
5
6
7
8

And then there
was my
nose.
It grew
BIGGER
and
BIGGER!

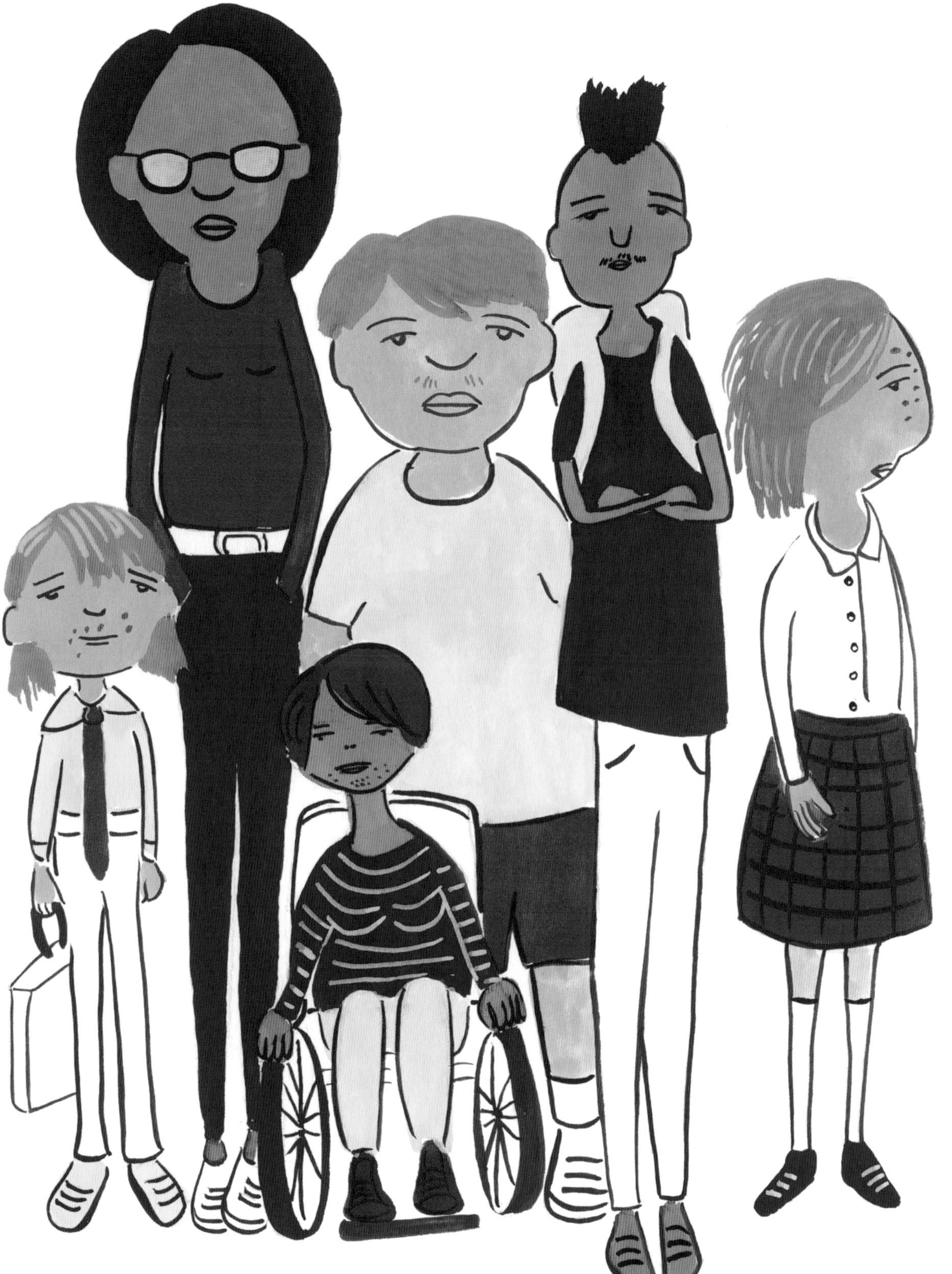

My only comfort was that others were going through their versions of the same thing. It was a hellish time for everyone — except for Gracie, whose puberty hell was mercifully quick. She gave us hope that one day we would also blossom from ugly ducklings into gorgeous swans.

Most of the time I flew under the radar, moving through the world unnoticed.

But every once in a while someone would pick on me and zero in on the obvious.

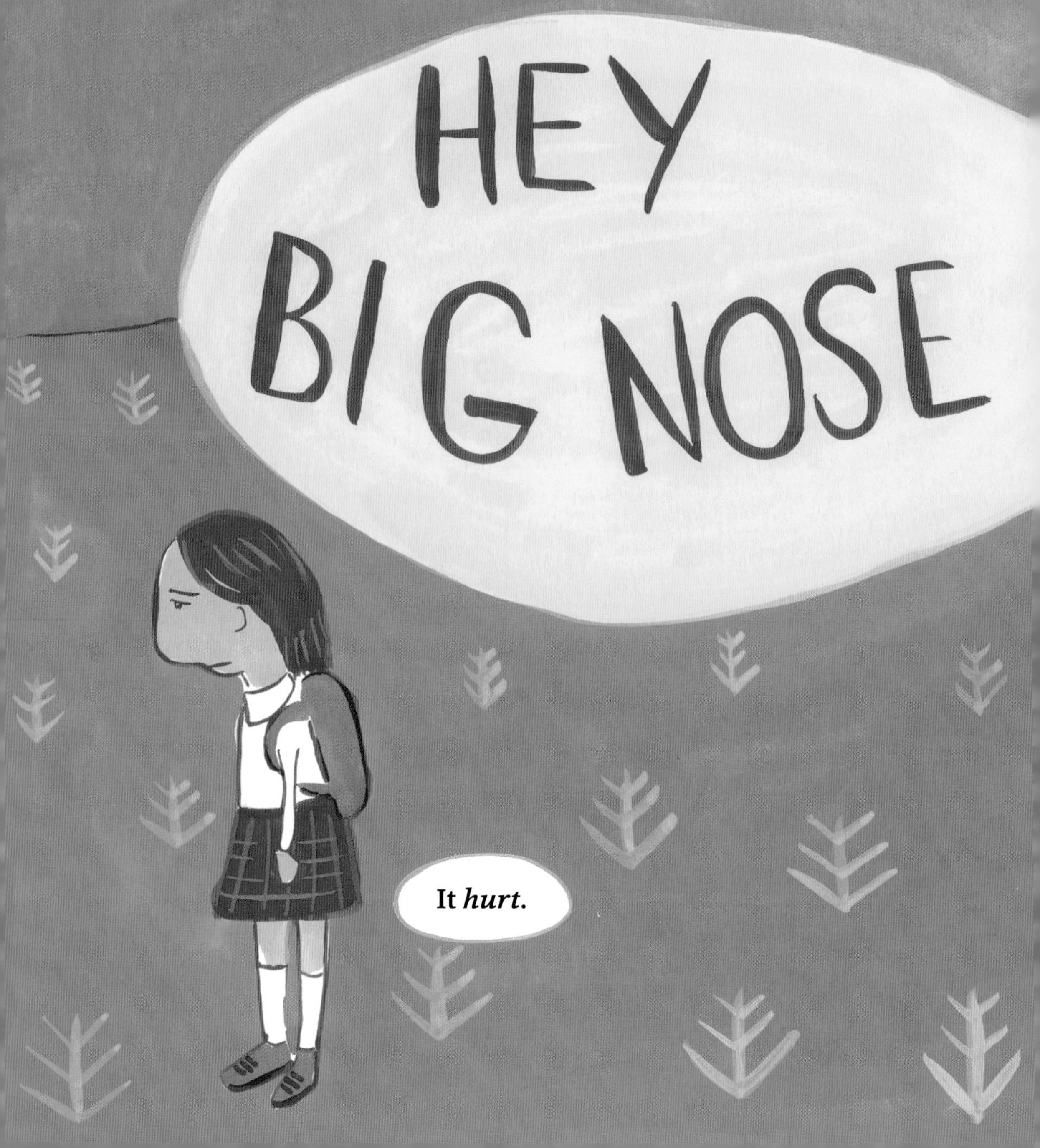
HEY BIG NOSE

It *hurt*.

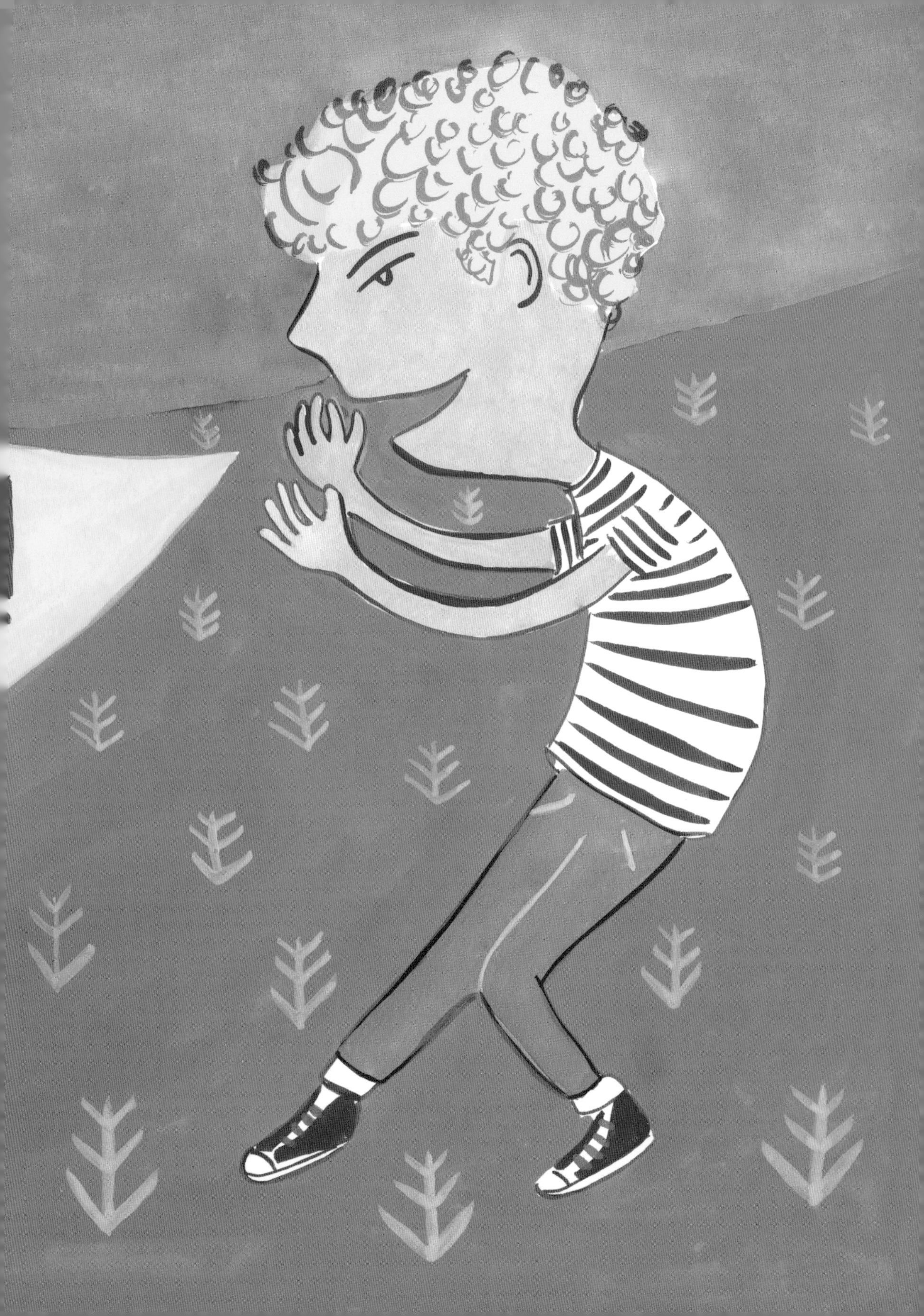

I had a special bond with a girl in my class named Belinda.

Our birthdays were one day apart and our mothers met while they were in the hospital. She wasn't my closest friend but she was, technically, my oldest.

Another thing: Belinda also had a big nose.

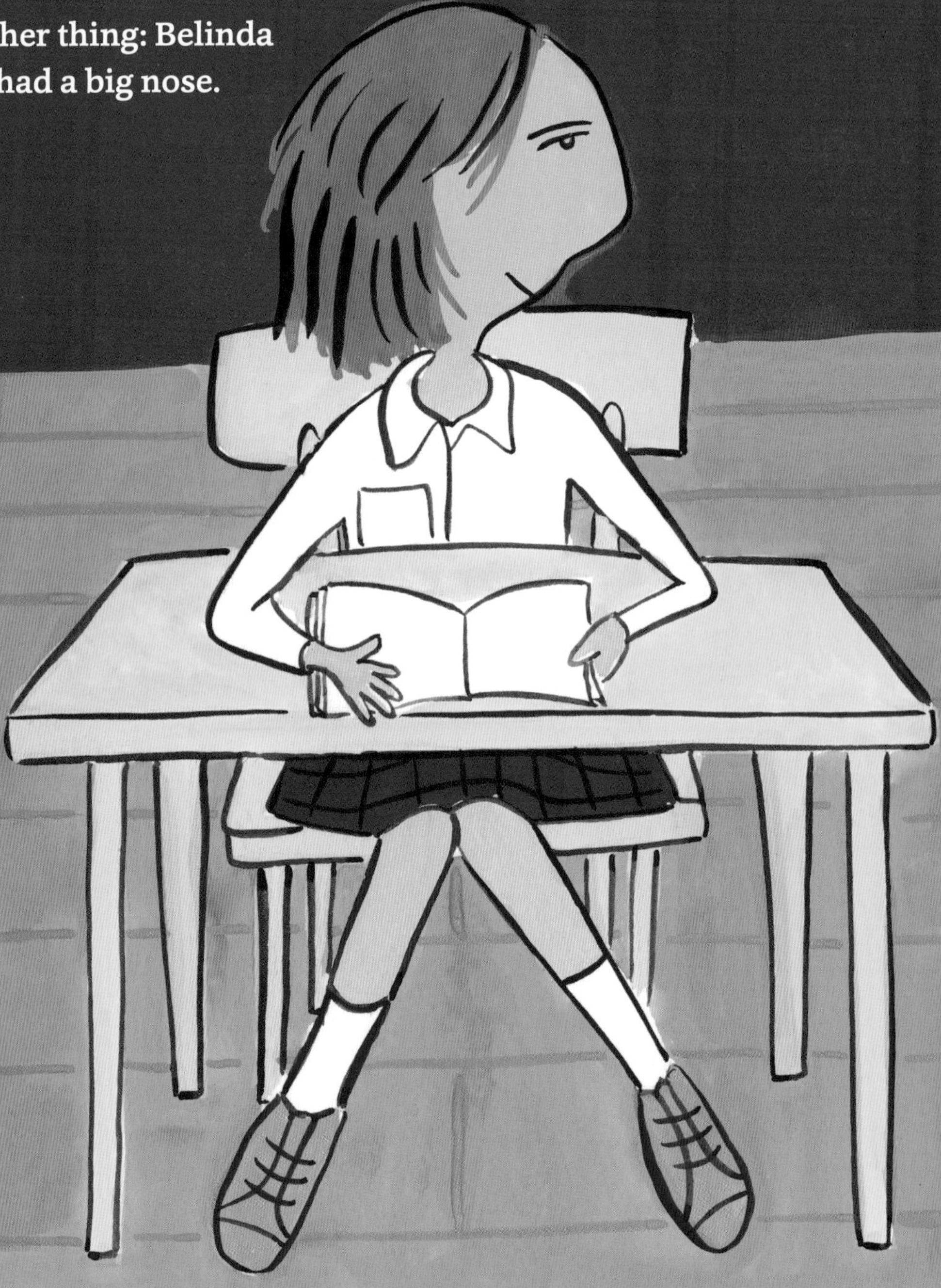

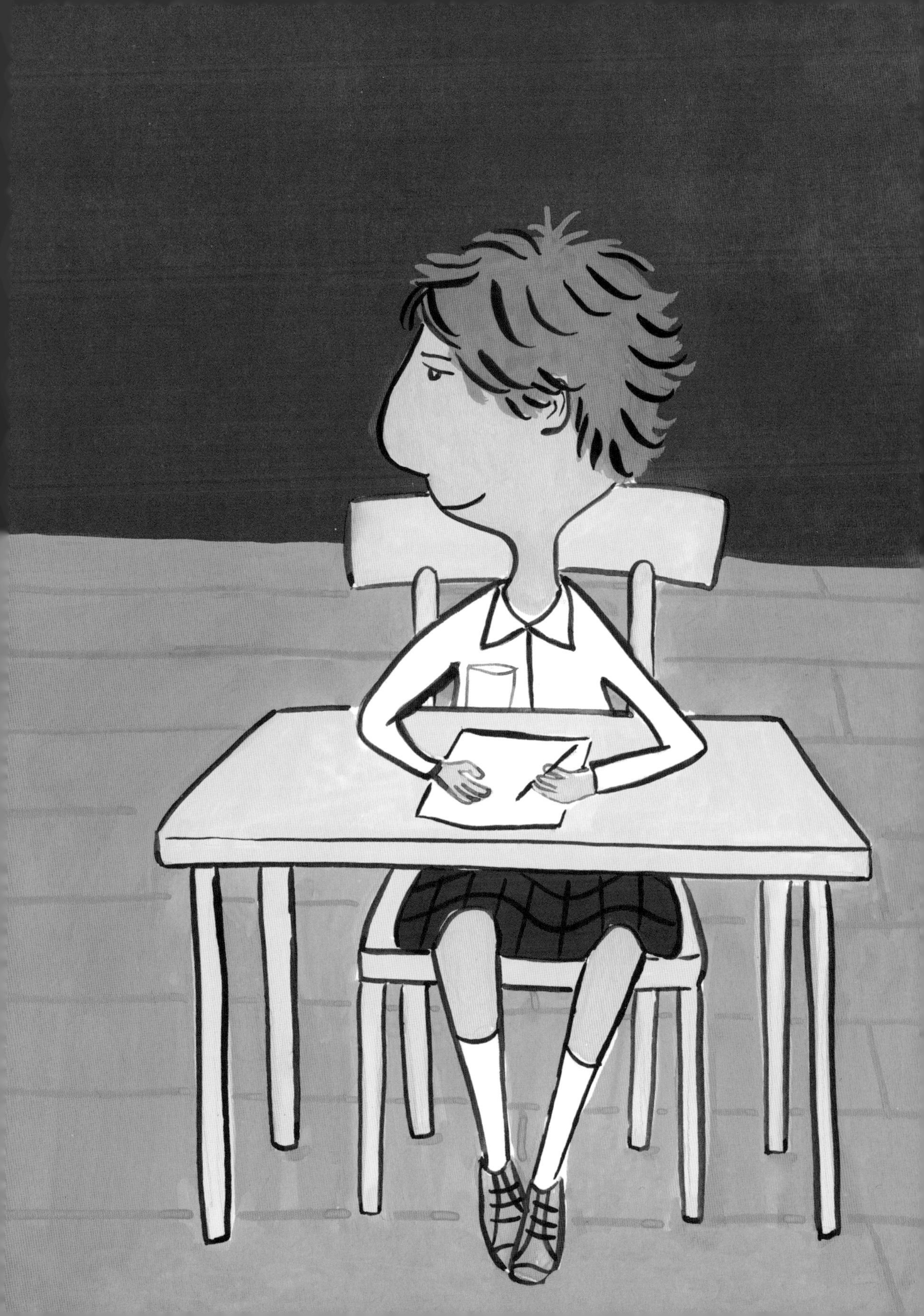

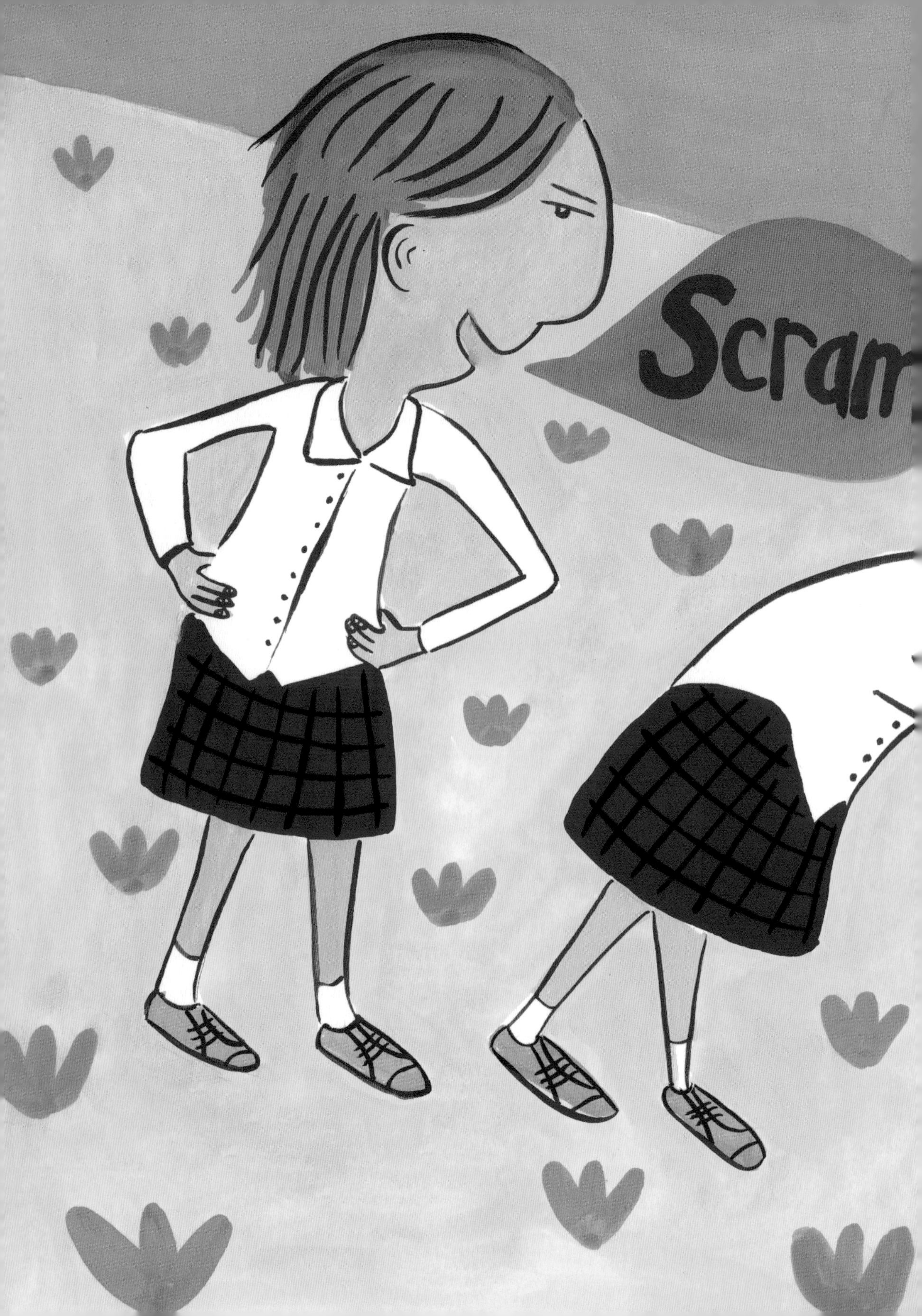
Scram

Belinda and I (and our big noses) were strong together.

It felt good to have a friend who shared the same pain.

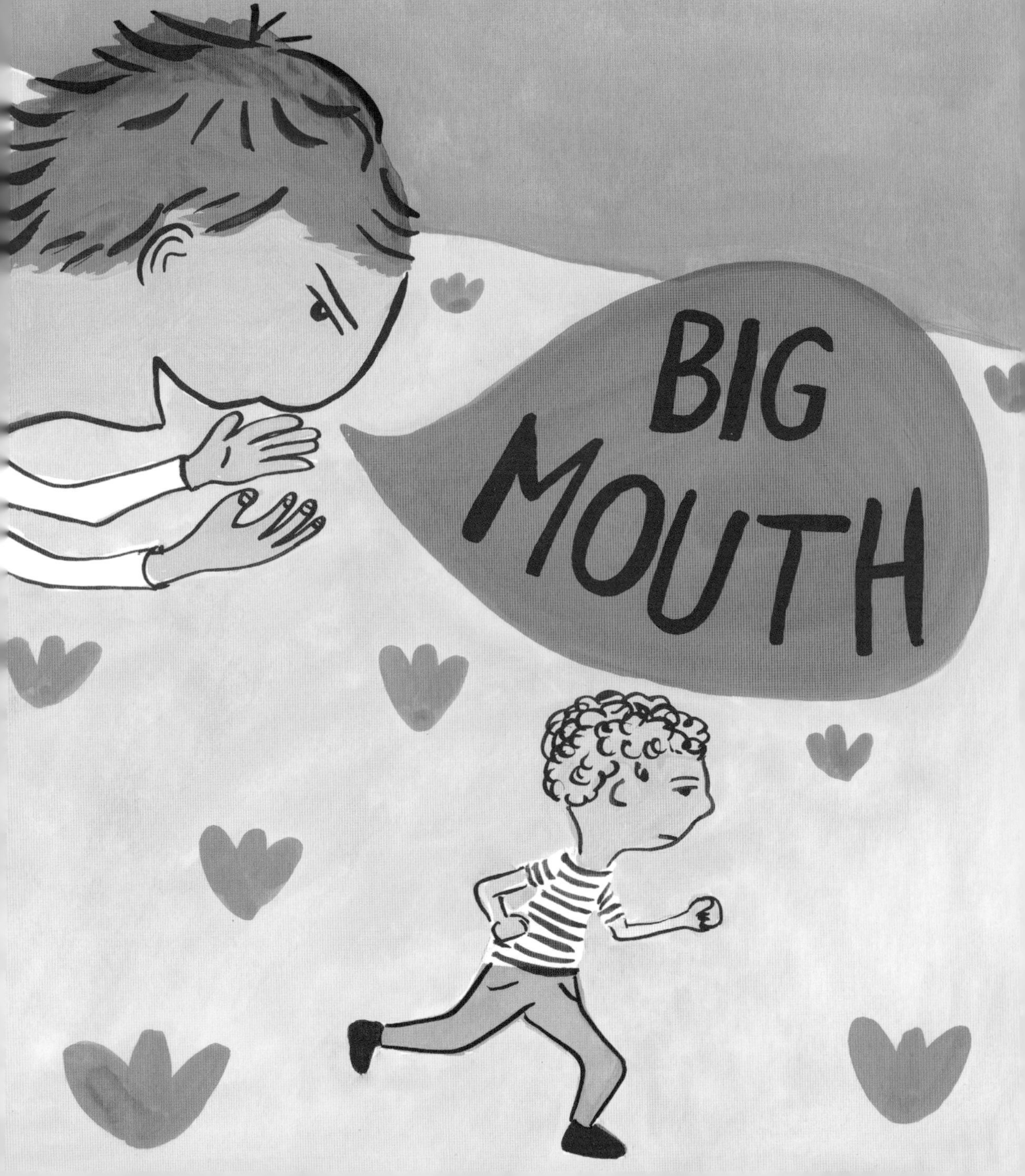
BIG MOUTH

On the first day of grade 9 while everyone was moving into their assigned lockers, I heard the familiar voice of a friend.

"Hey, we're beside each other!" the voice said happily.

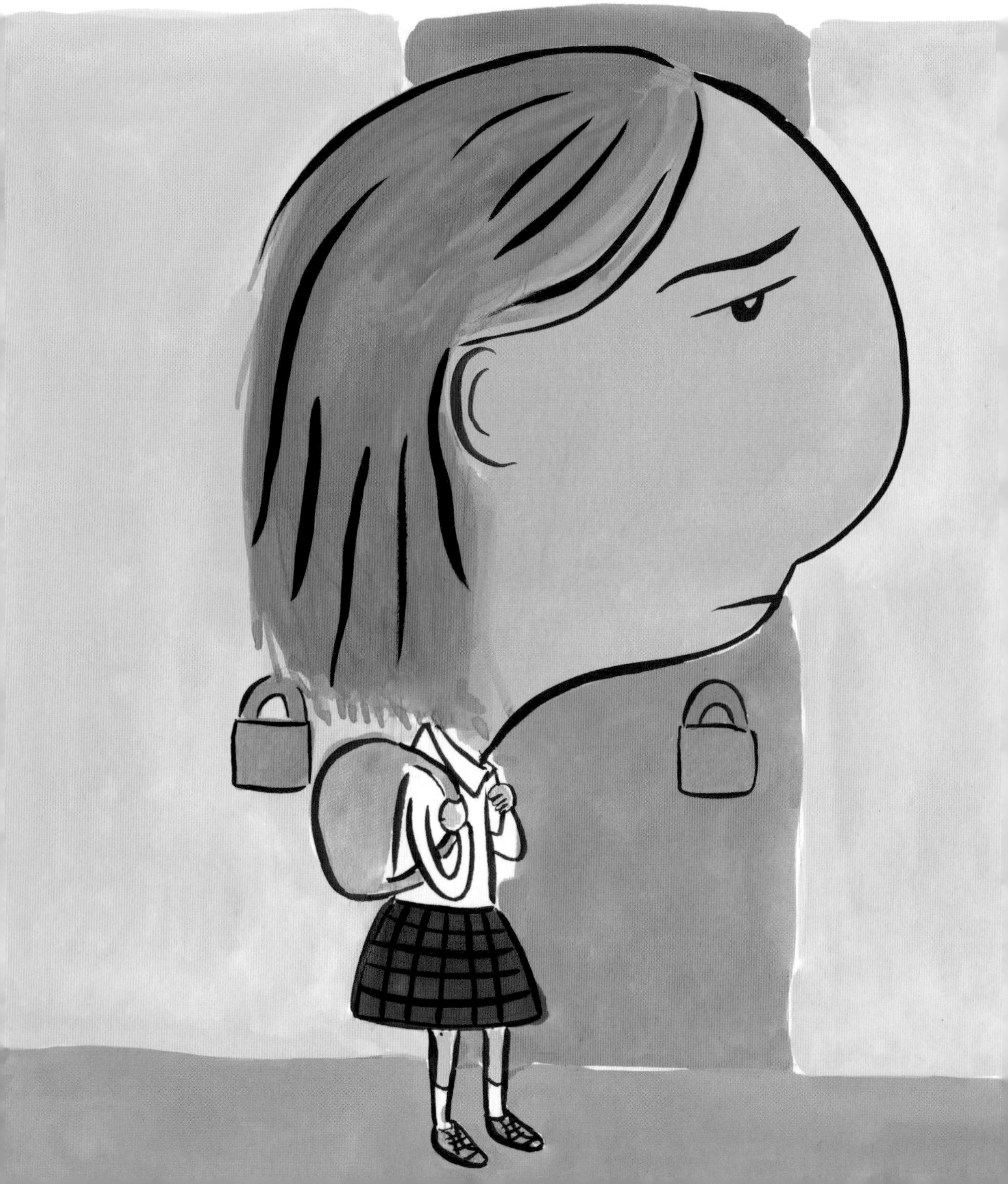

I searched the room to see who the voice was coming from, but I didn't recognize her ... And then, I did. The happy voice was Belinda's — but it wasn't coming from the Belinda I knew. Her formerly big nose was now small and turned up. Belinda had gotten a nose job. I felt betrayed.

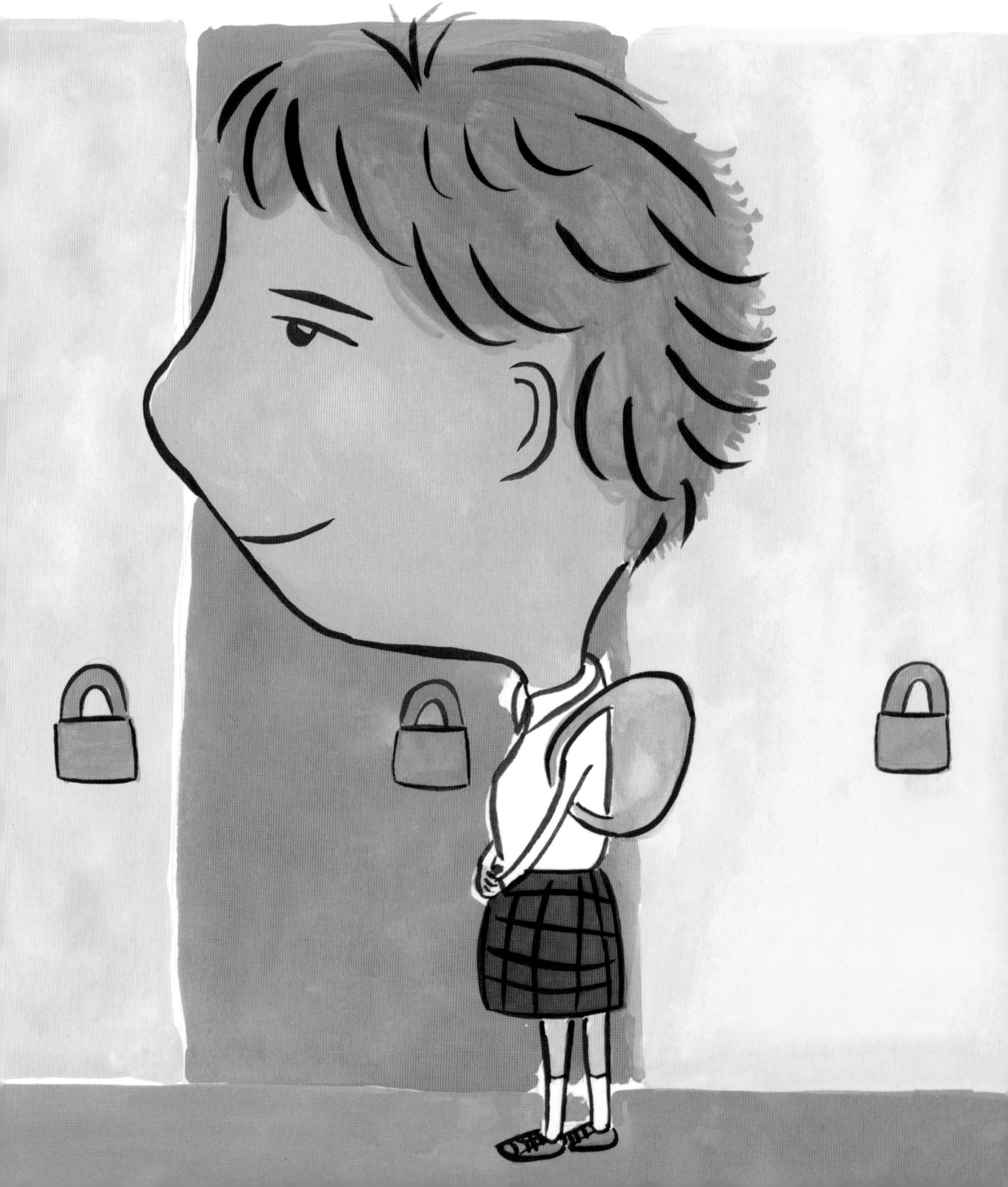

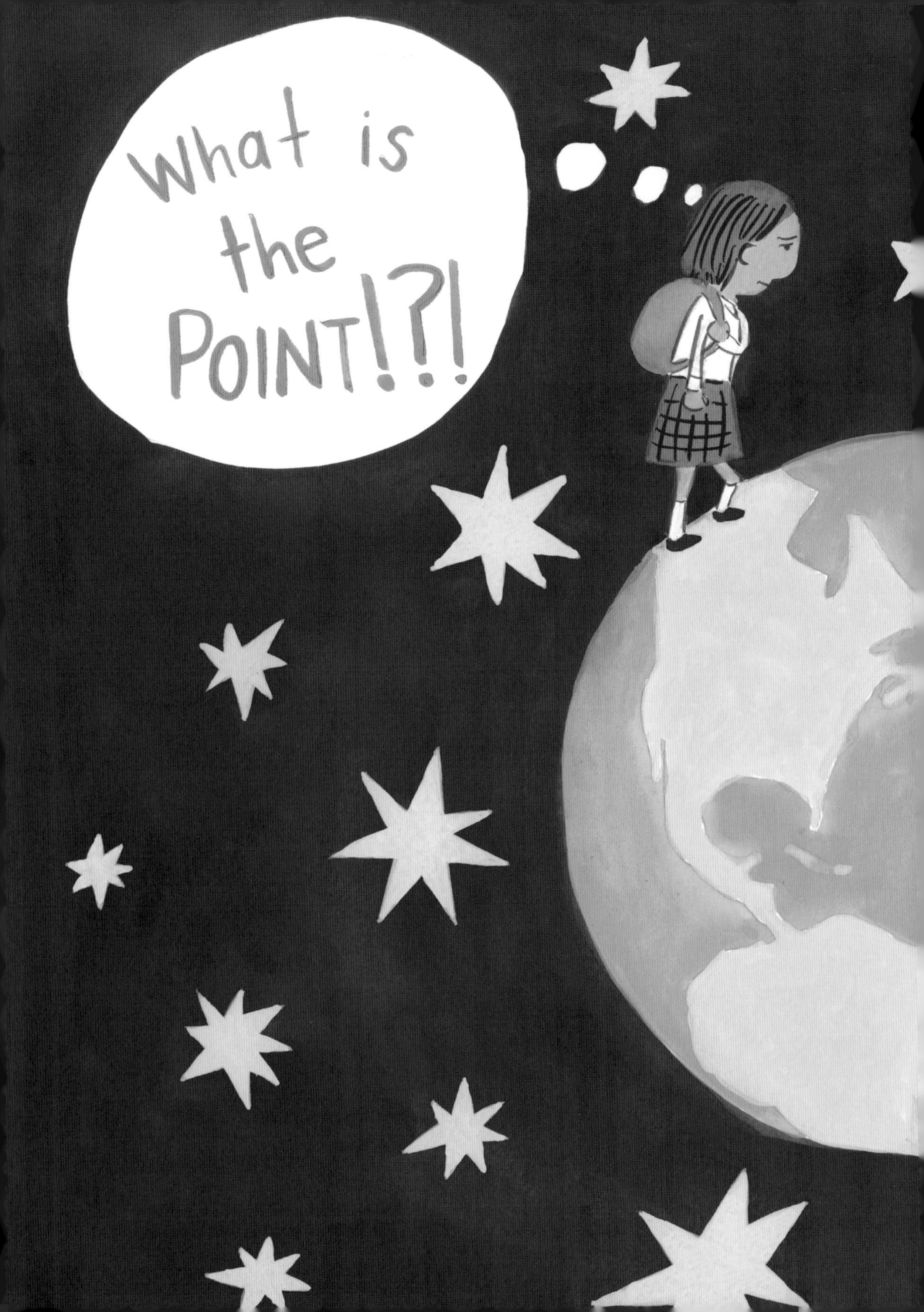
What is the POINT!?!

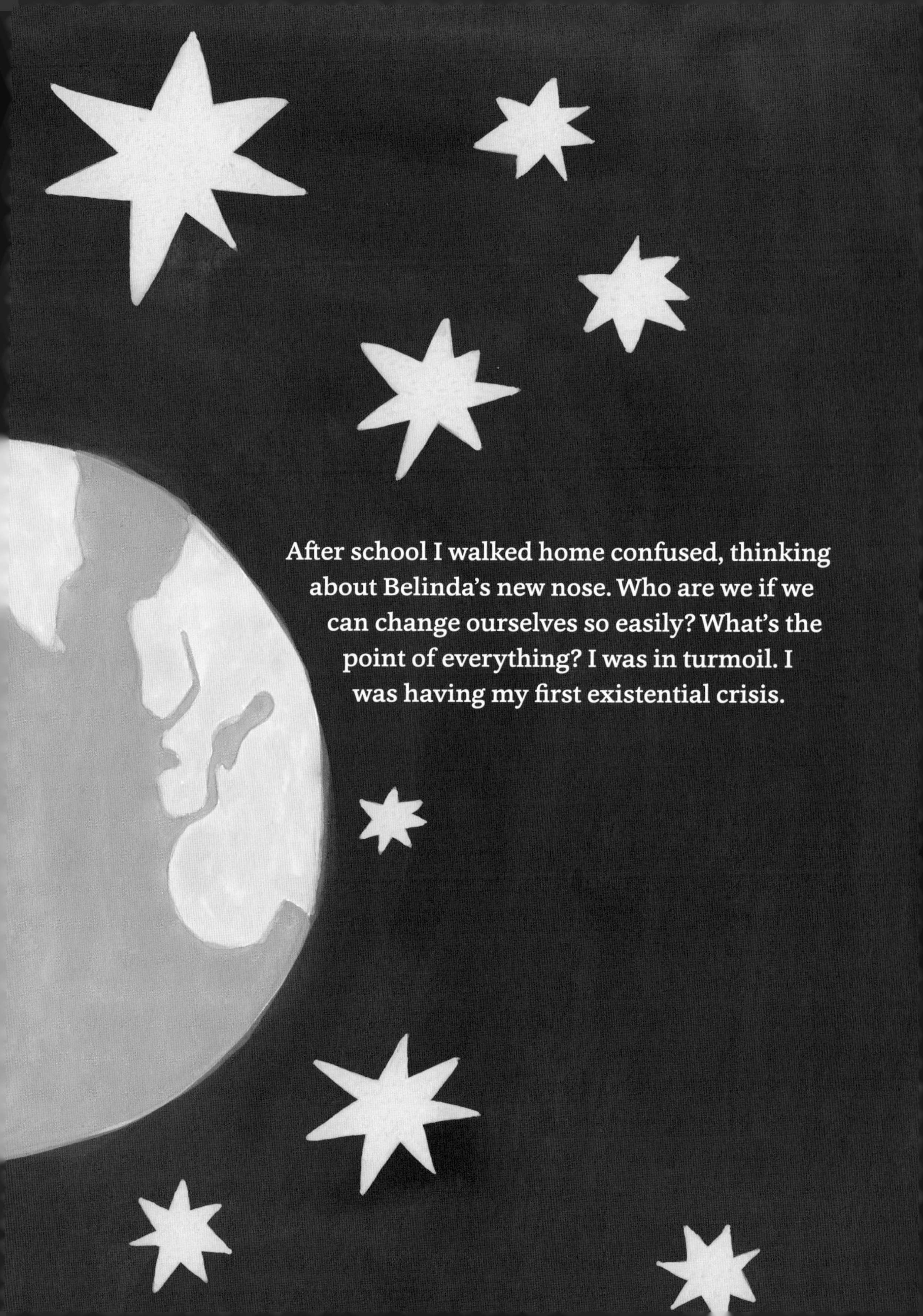

After school I walked home confused, thinking about Belinda's new nose. Who are we if we can change ourselves so easily? What's the point of everything? I was in turmoil. I was having my first existential crisis.

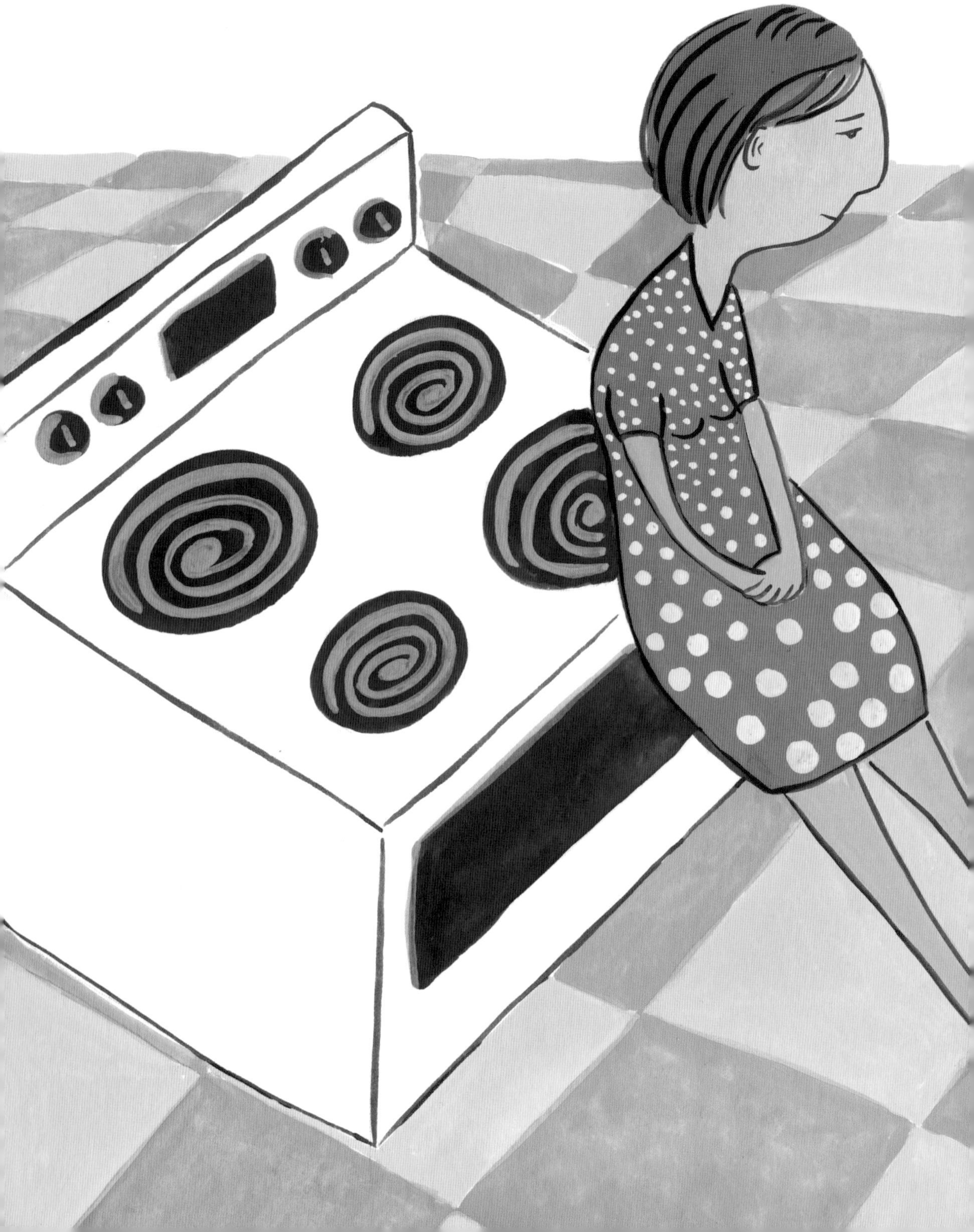

When I got home I told my mother about Belinda's nose job. From the look on her face I could tell that she already knew about it. I could also tell that she felt terrible for me. She asked, "Do you want a nose job too?"

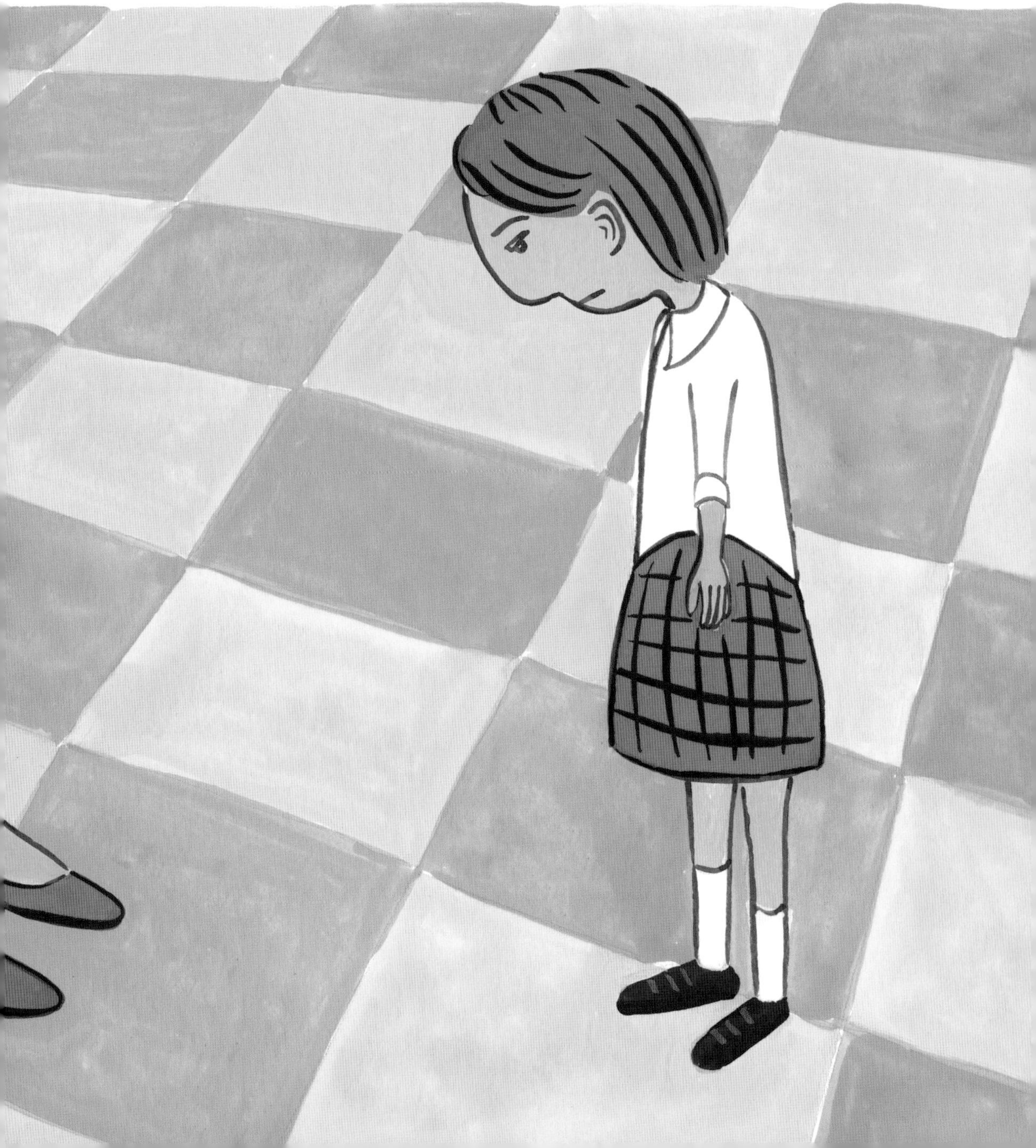

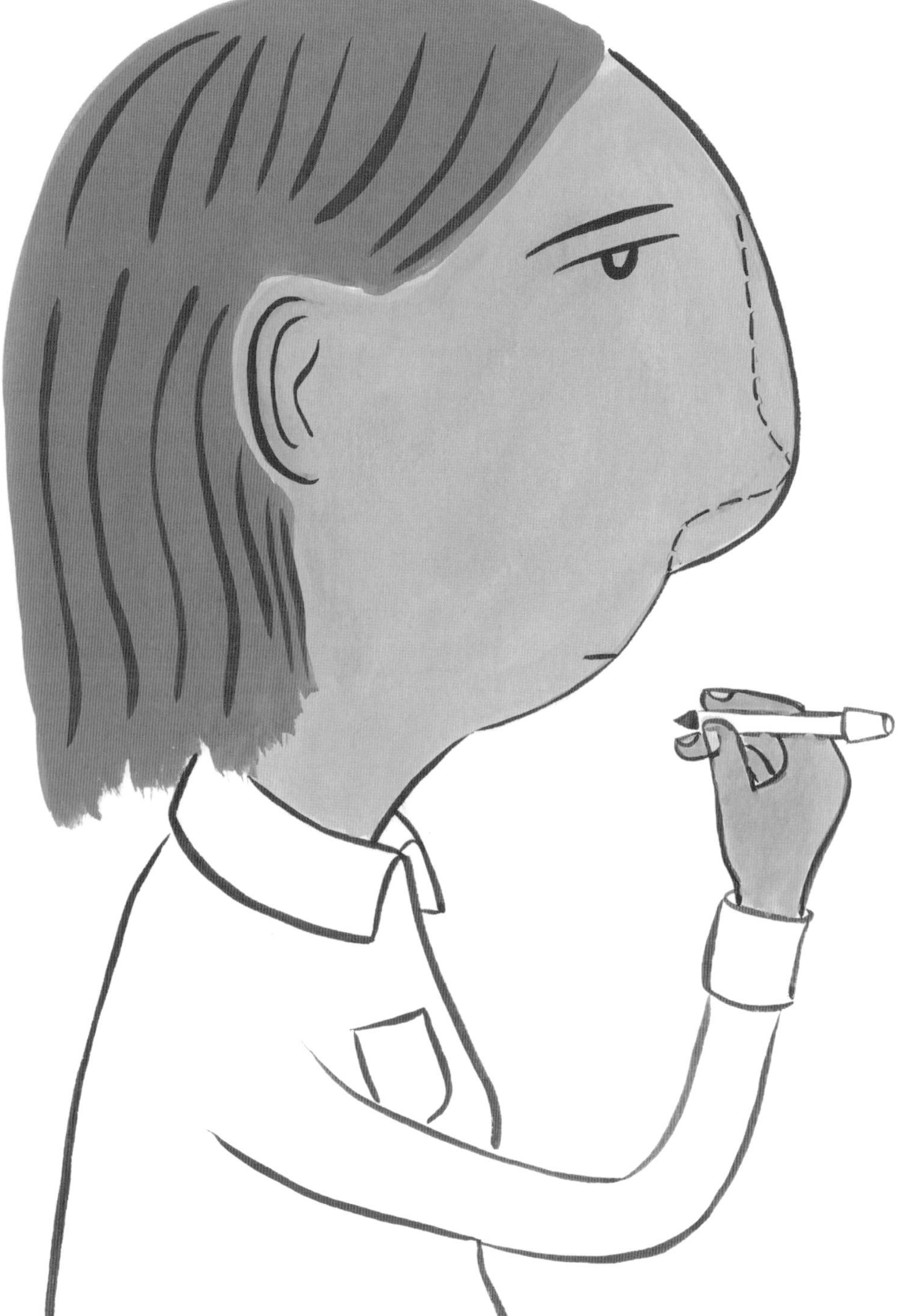

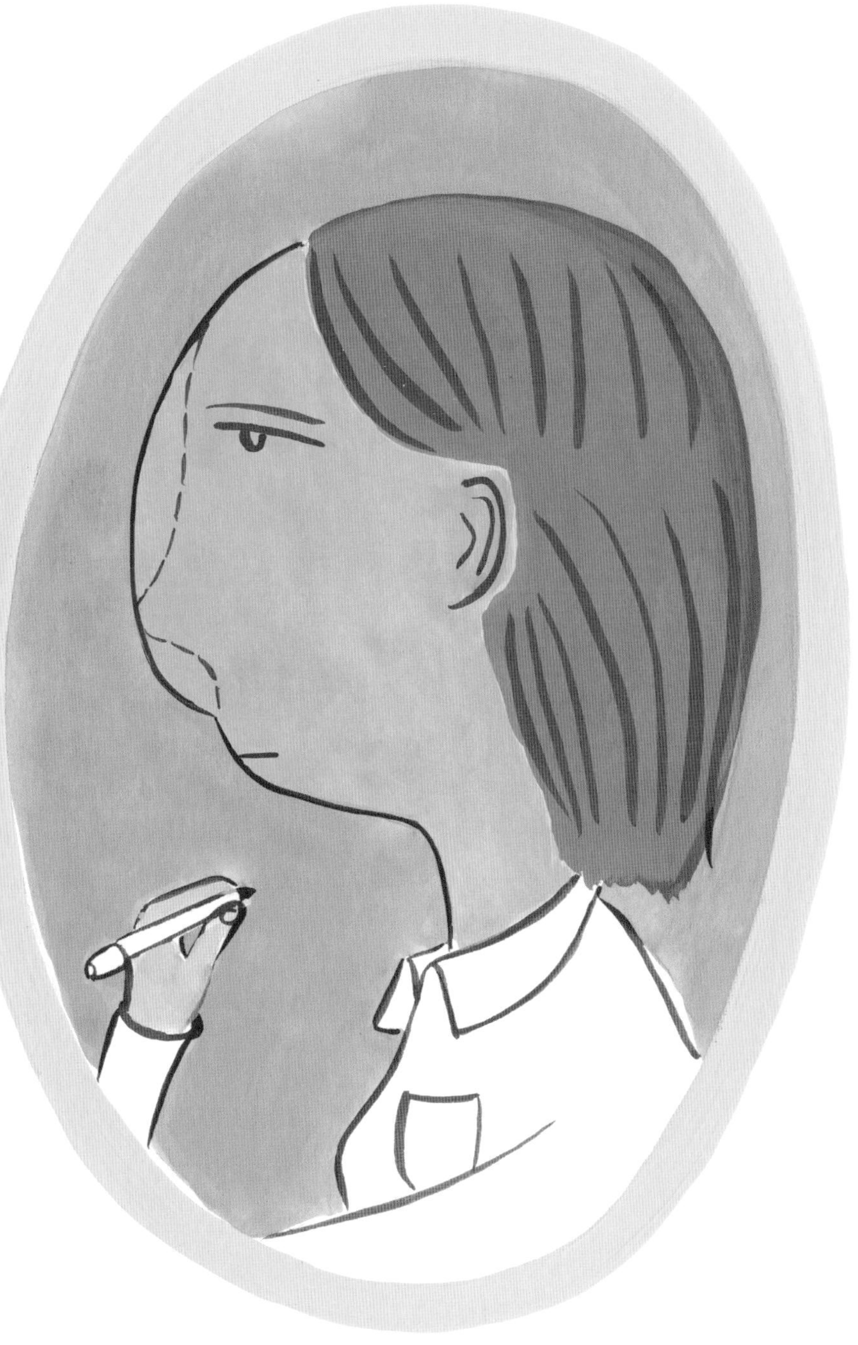

I thought about what my mother had asked. Could a nose job change my life? Would it transform me from an ugly duckling into a gorgeous swan? Looking at my face from different angles, I drew a dotted line down the bridge of my nose and imagined that a surgeon could follow it to create a new one. I examined my nose. Could I change it?

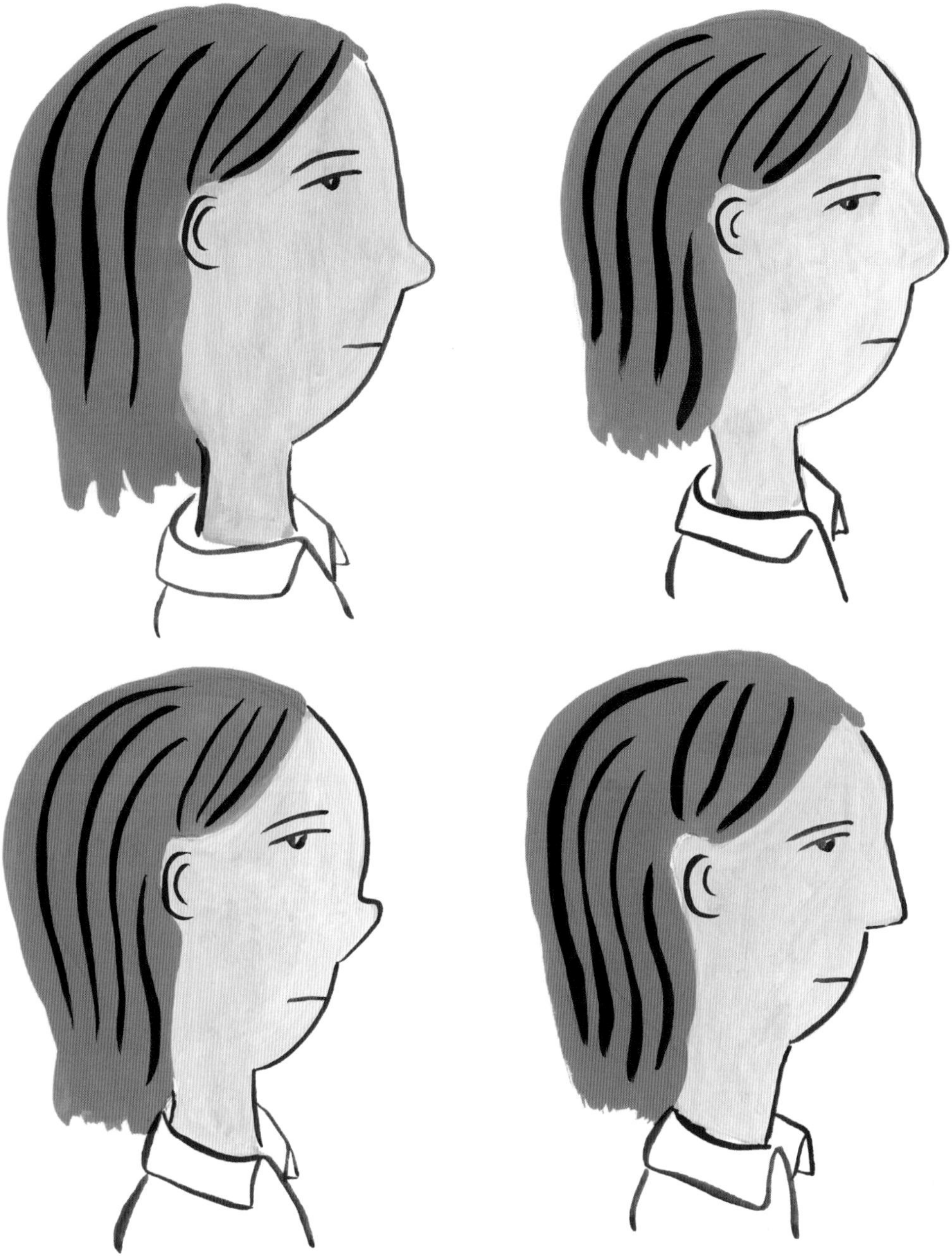

But if I changed this part of me, then who would I be? This big question scared me. Getting a nose job scared me. I decided that no matter how big my nose got, I couldn't change it because my nose was me. I was my nose.

I also decided I was flawed.

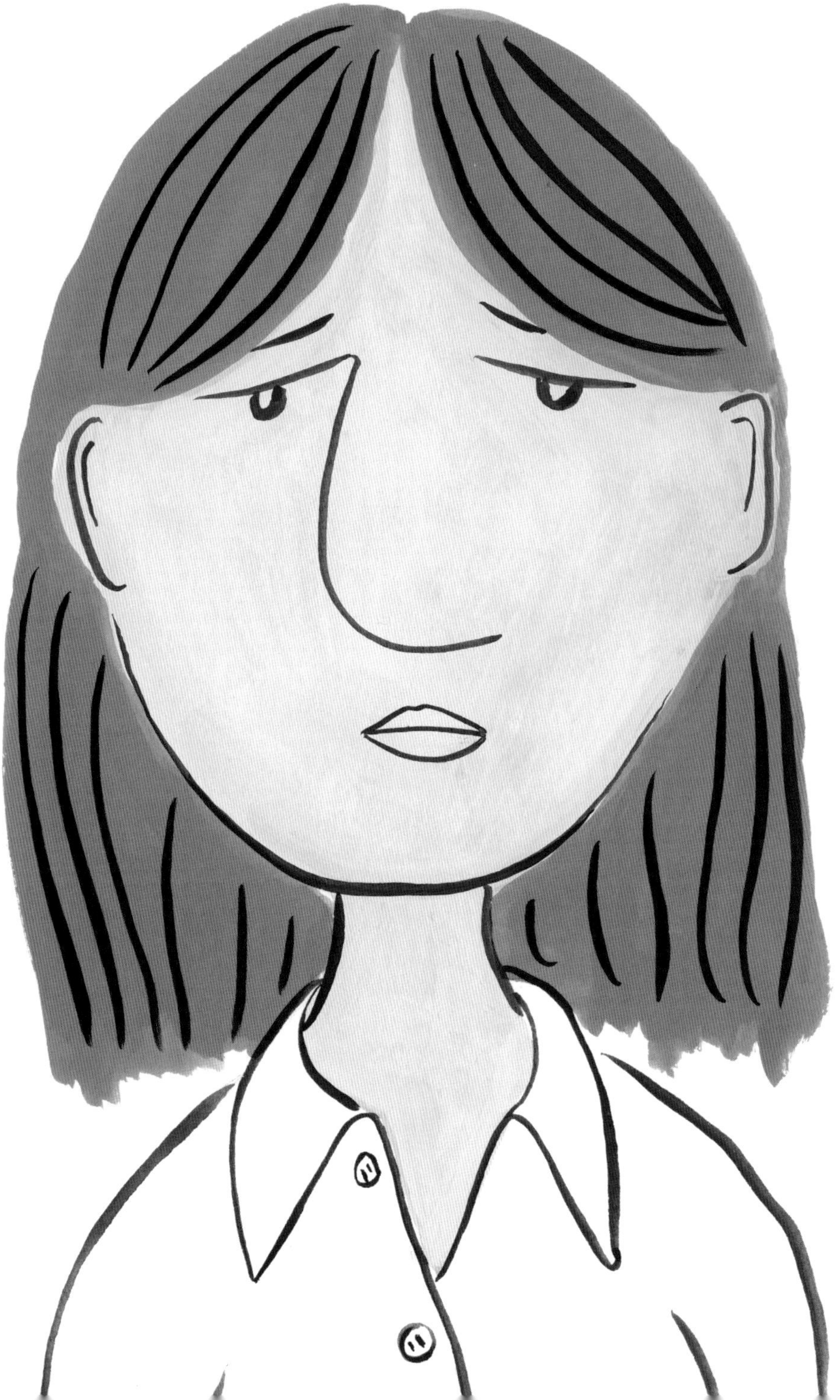

For years I pretended my big nose didn't bother me, but it did and I hated the way it looked.

I blamed Belinda for getting a nose job and deserting me. I blamed cosmetic surgery for making me feel like there was a right kind of nose. I blamed the advertising industry for making women feel like there was an ideal beauty. I blamed the world for making women feel like they should be a certain way.

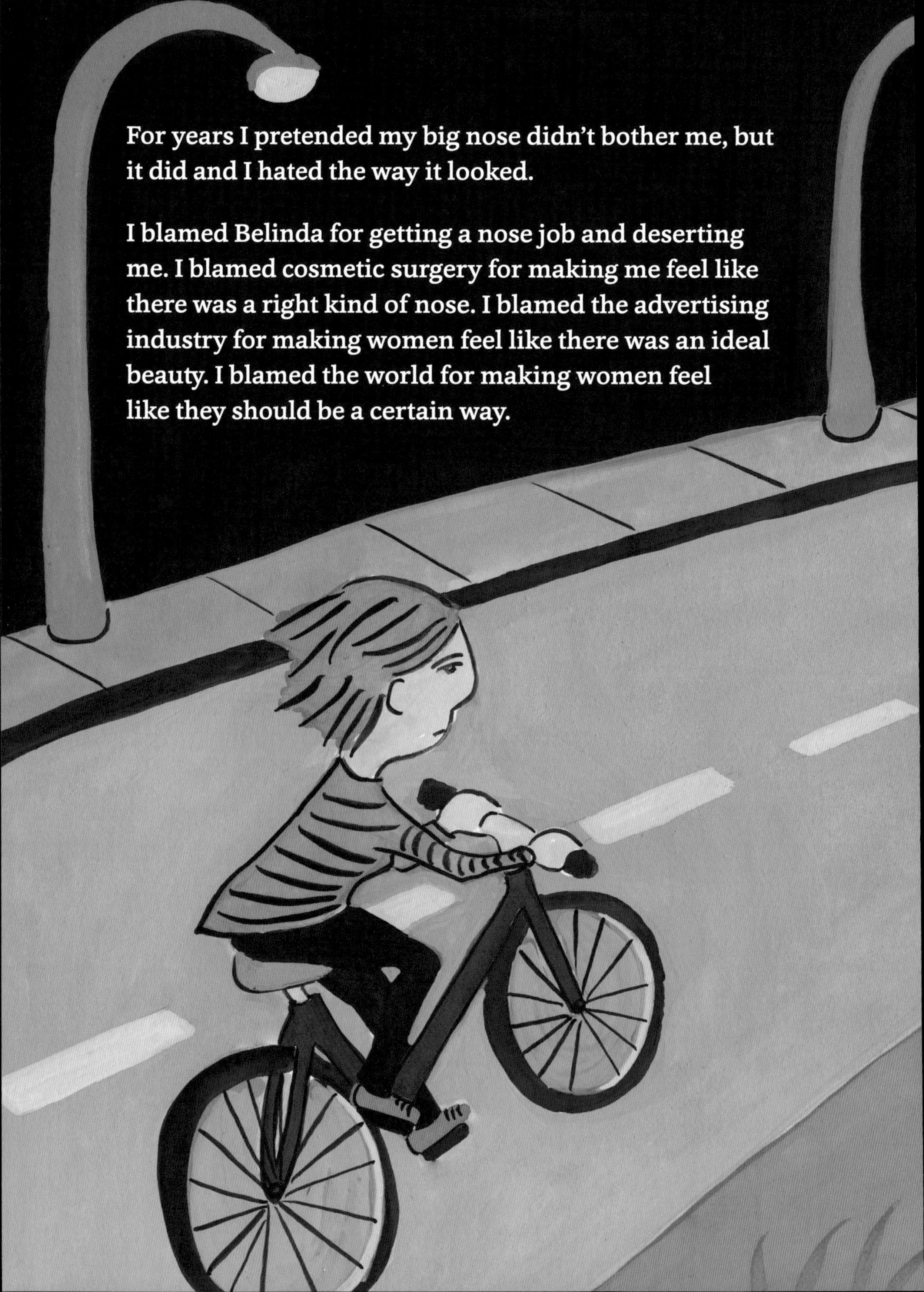

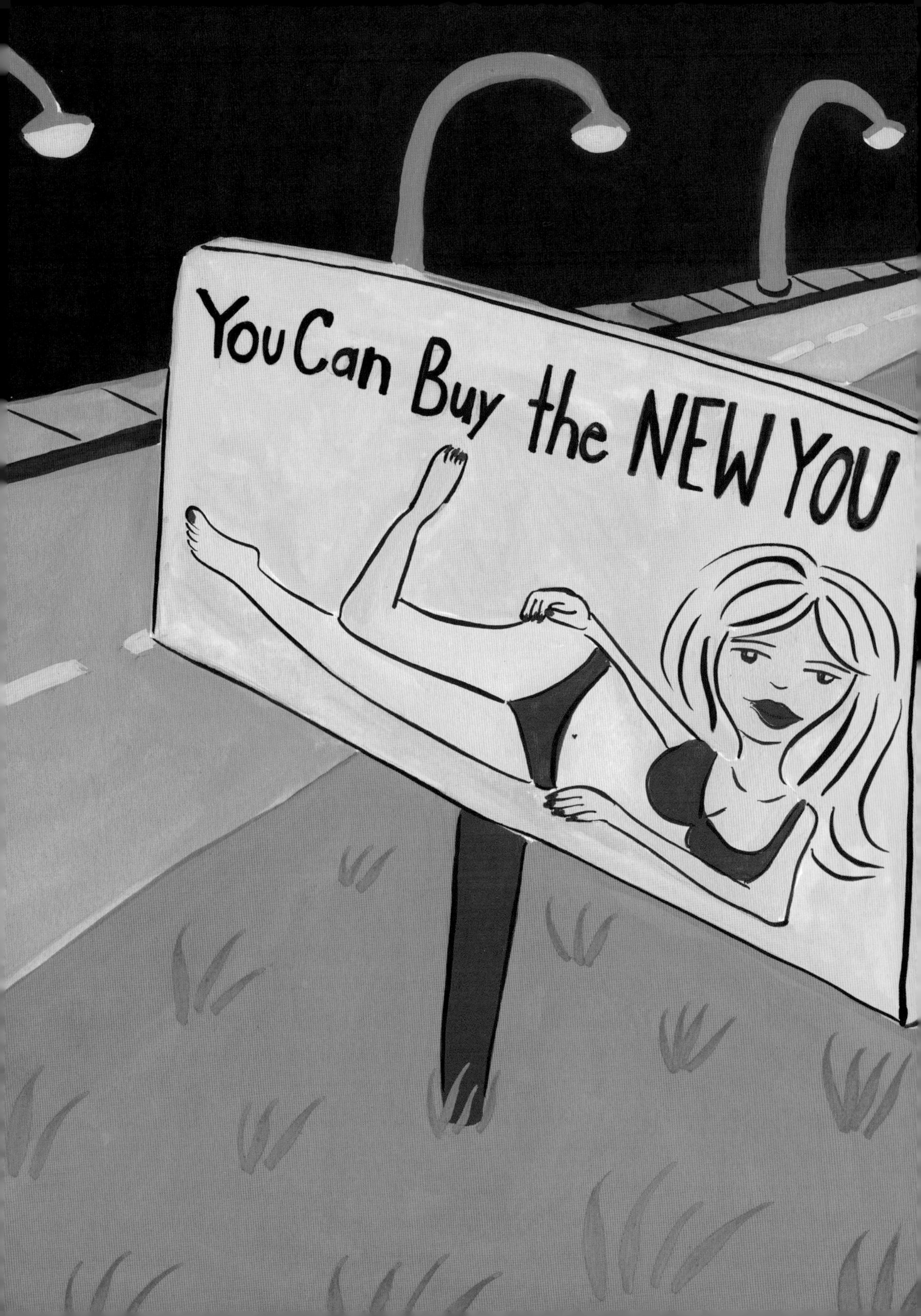
You Can Buy the NEW YOU

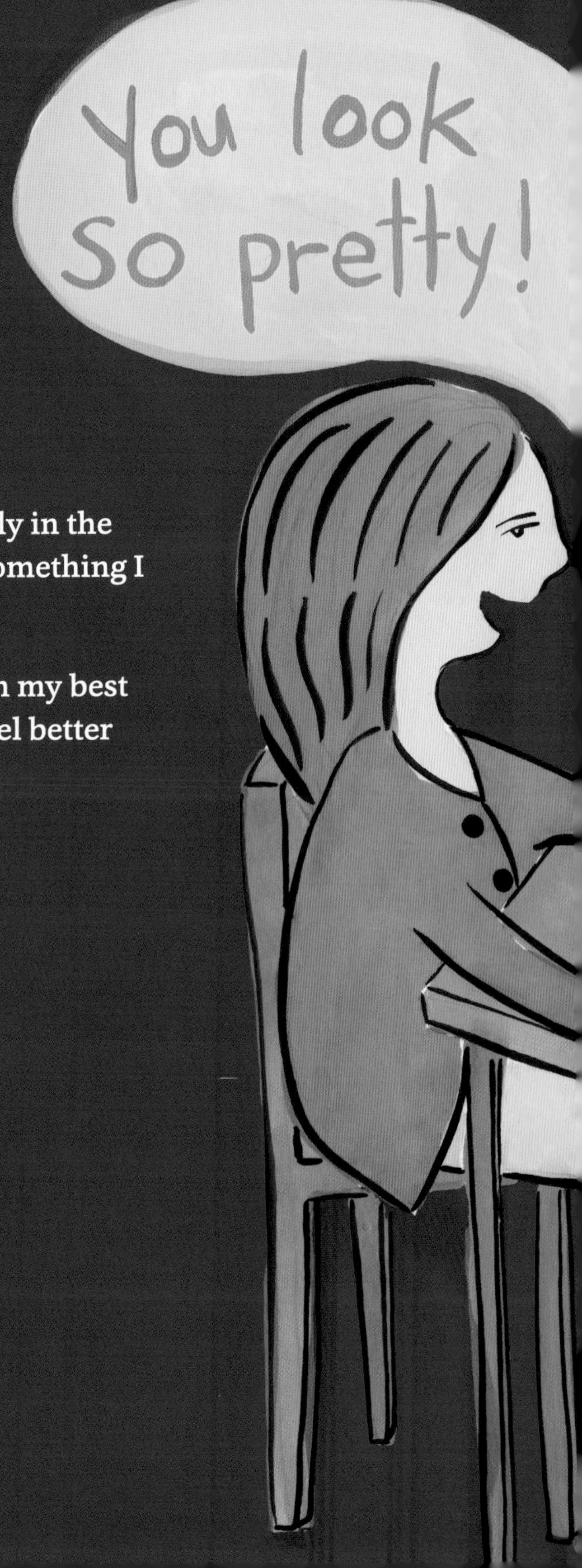
You look So pretty!

My nose, located prominently in the center of my face, became something I couldn't talk about.

It embarrassed me, and even my best friends couldn't make me feel better about myself.

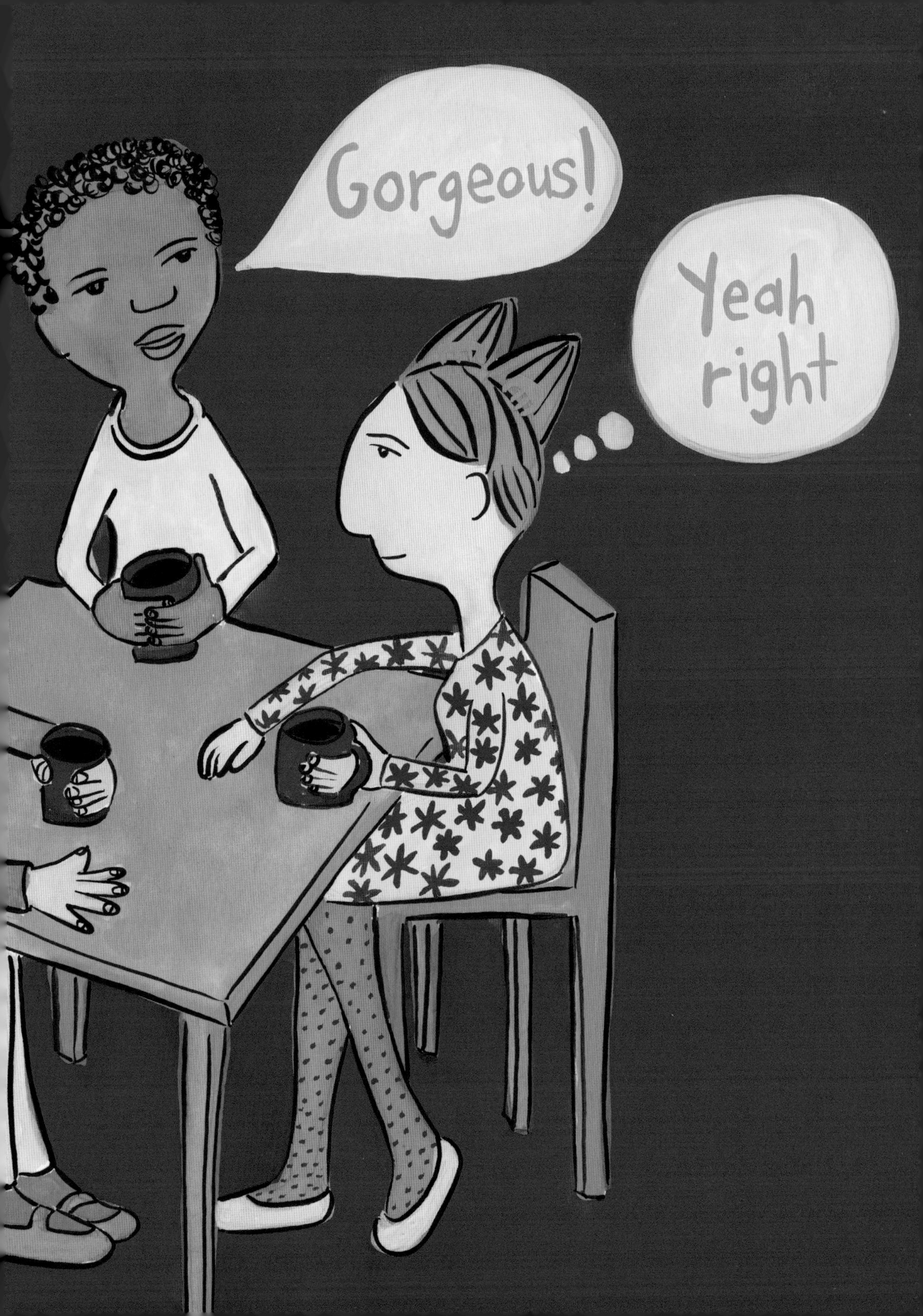
Gorgeous!
Yeah right

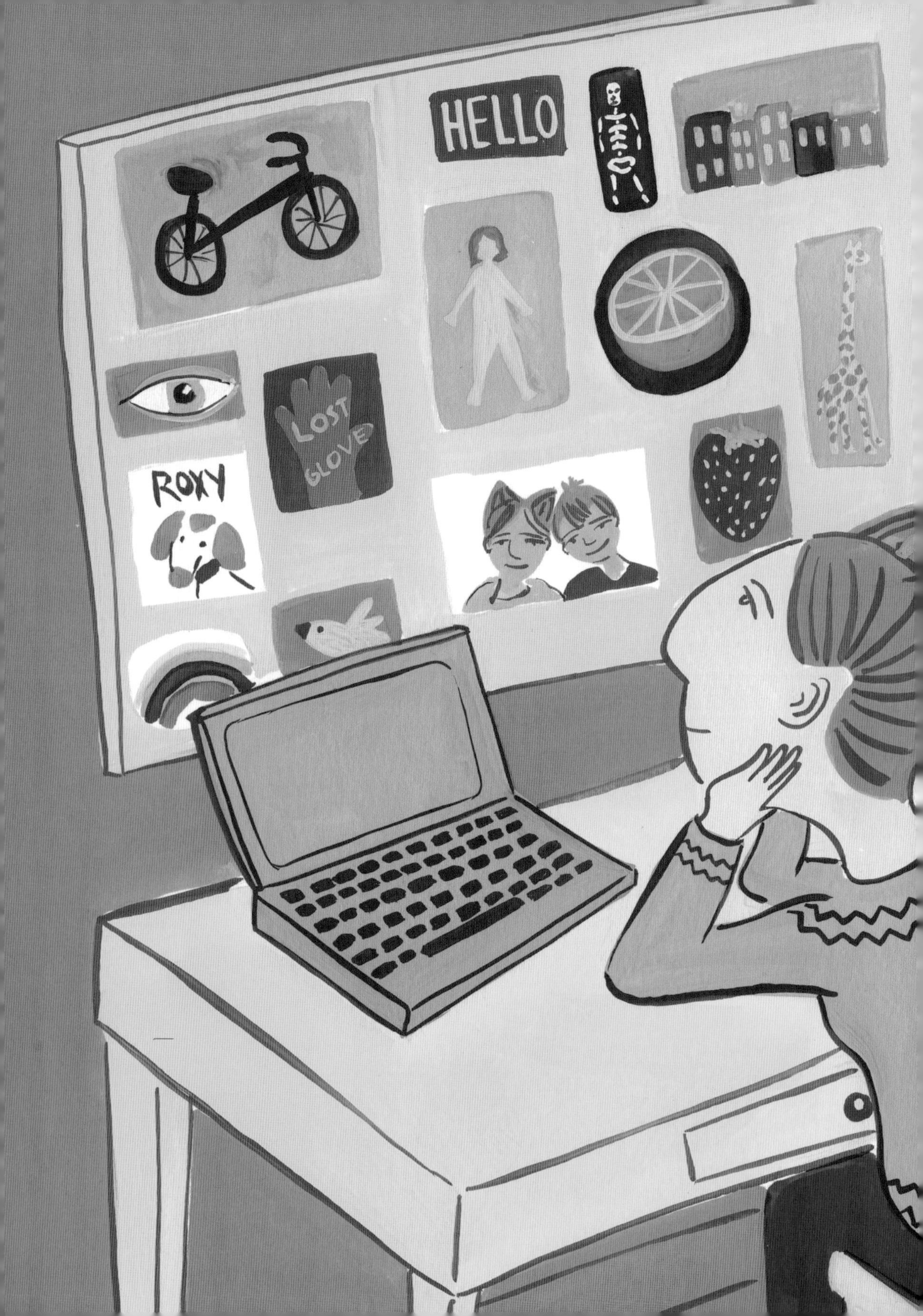
HELLO
LOST GLOVE
ROXY

And then I fell in love with a plastic surgeon, and I couldn't ignore my nose anymore.

Beautiful handmade postcards covered my bulletin board. Dave didn't consider himself an artist, but I was staring at a small exhibition's worth of exquisite artwork. The postcards were symbolic of Dave's courage to try something new, simply because I asked him to.

All this time I blamed plastic surgery (and by extension Dave) for feeling flawed.

But then I had an epiphany: I was the person who decided I was flawed and, therefore, I was the only person who could do something to change my point of view. I had an idea.

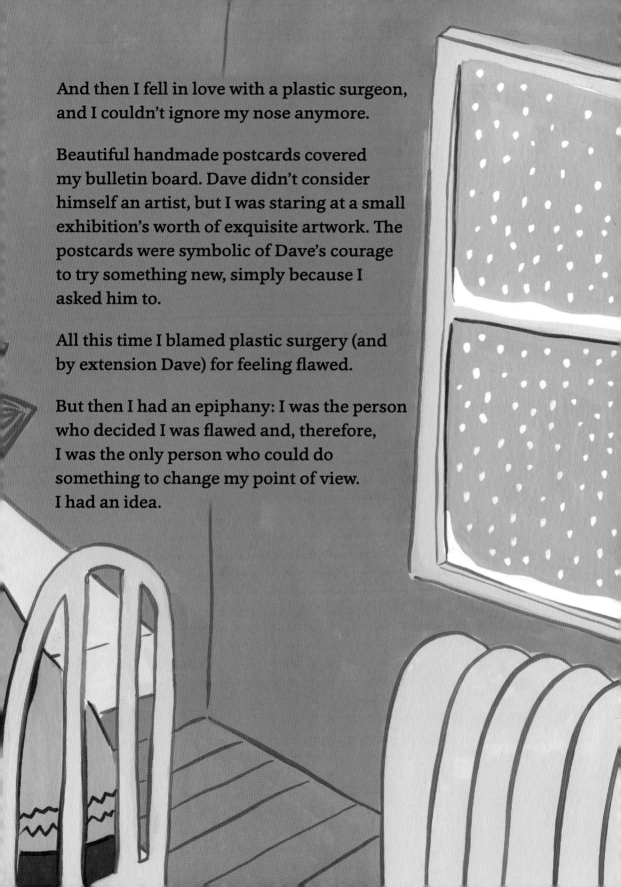

I called Dave.

"Our next postcard will be a secret. Something we've never told each other because we're afraid to talk about it."

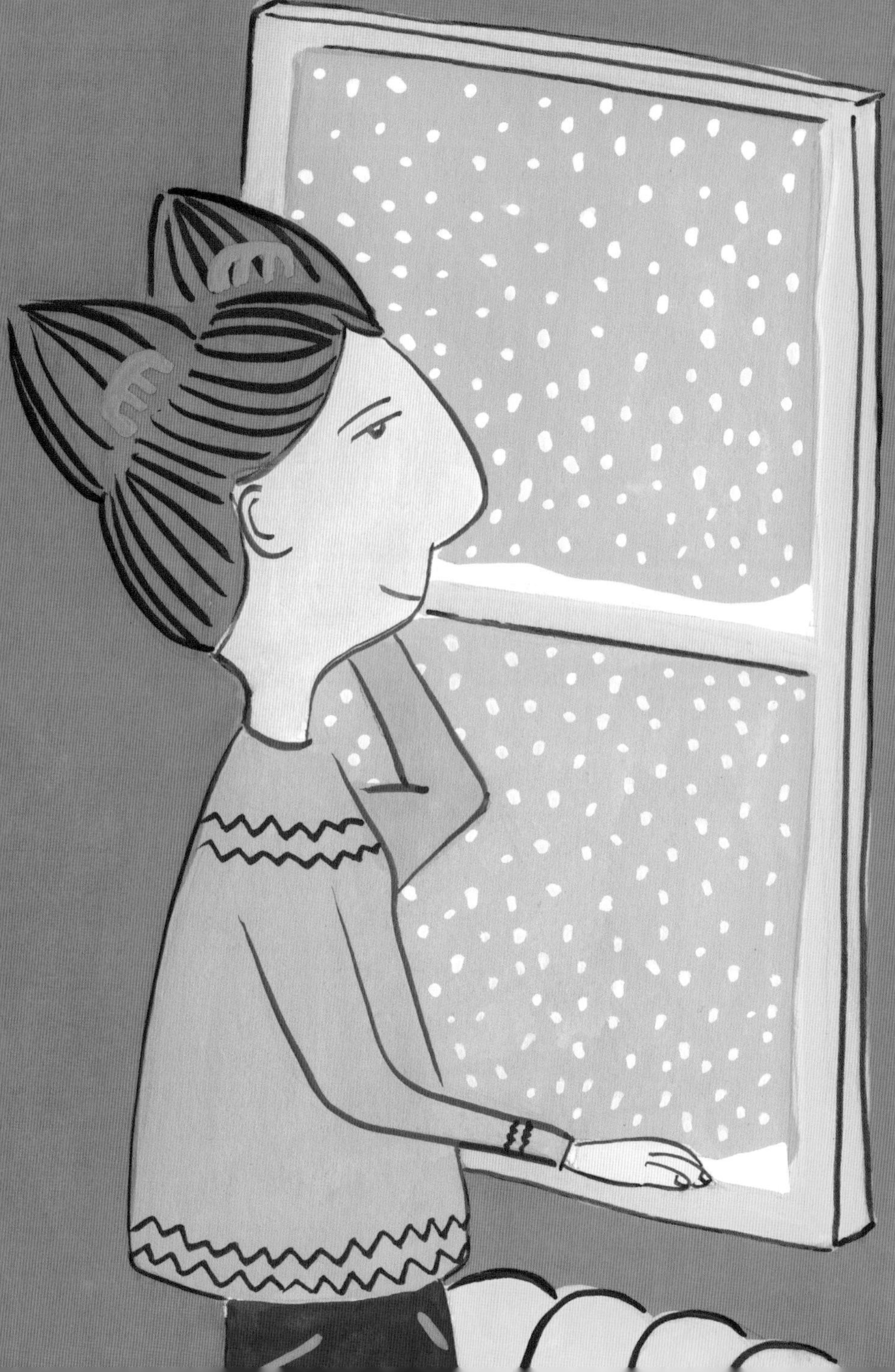

Dave thought about it for a moment. "Can we put this one in an envelope?"

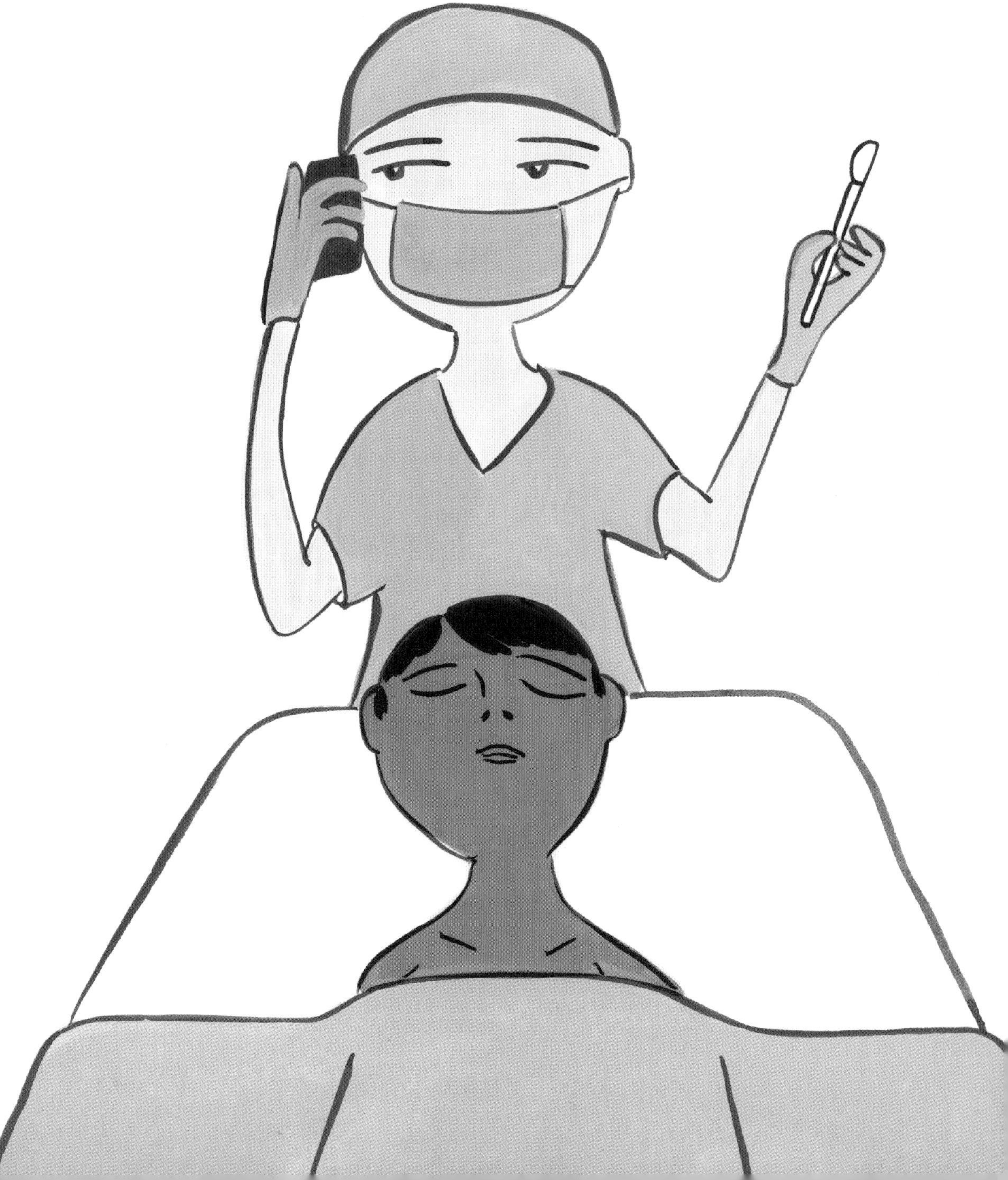

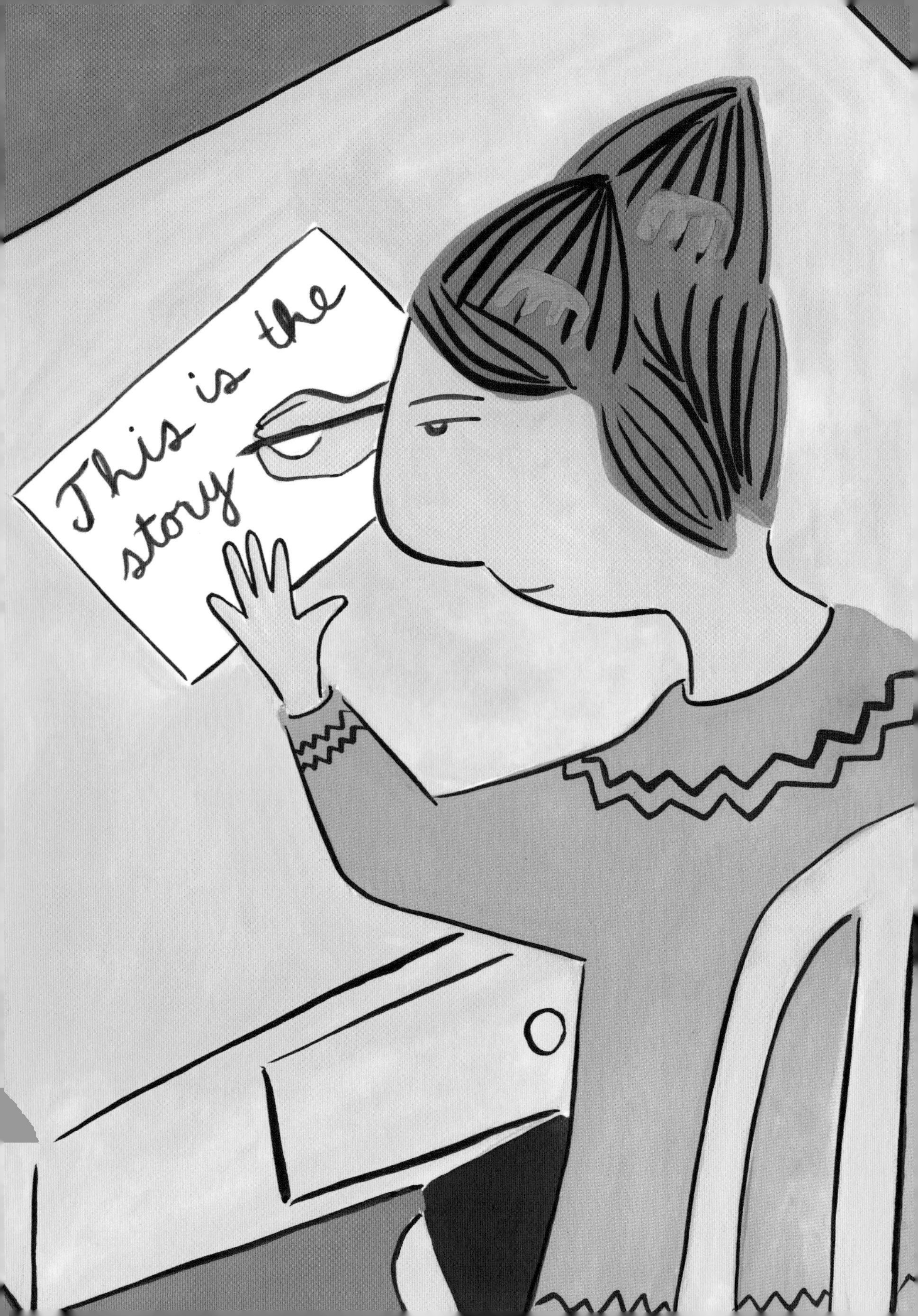
This is the story

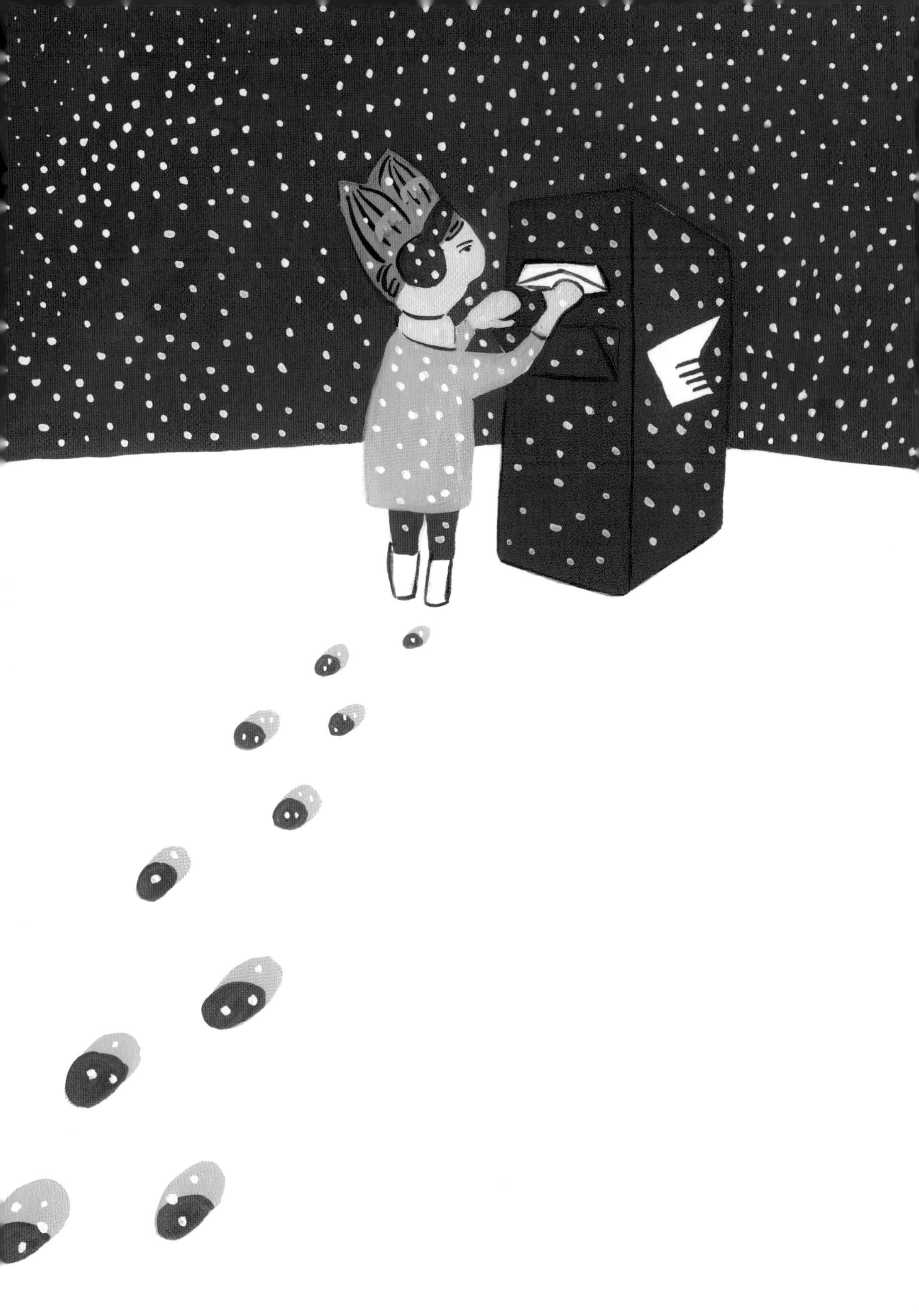

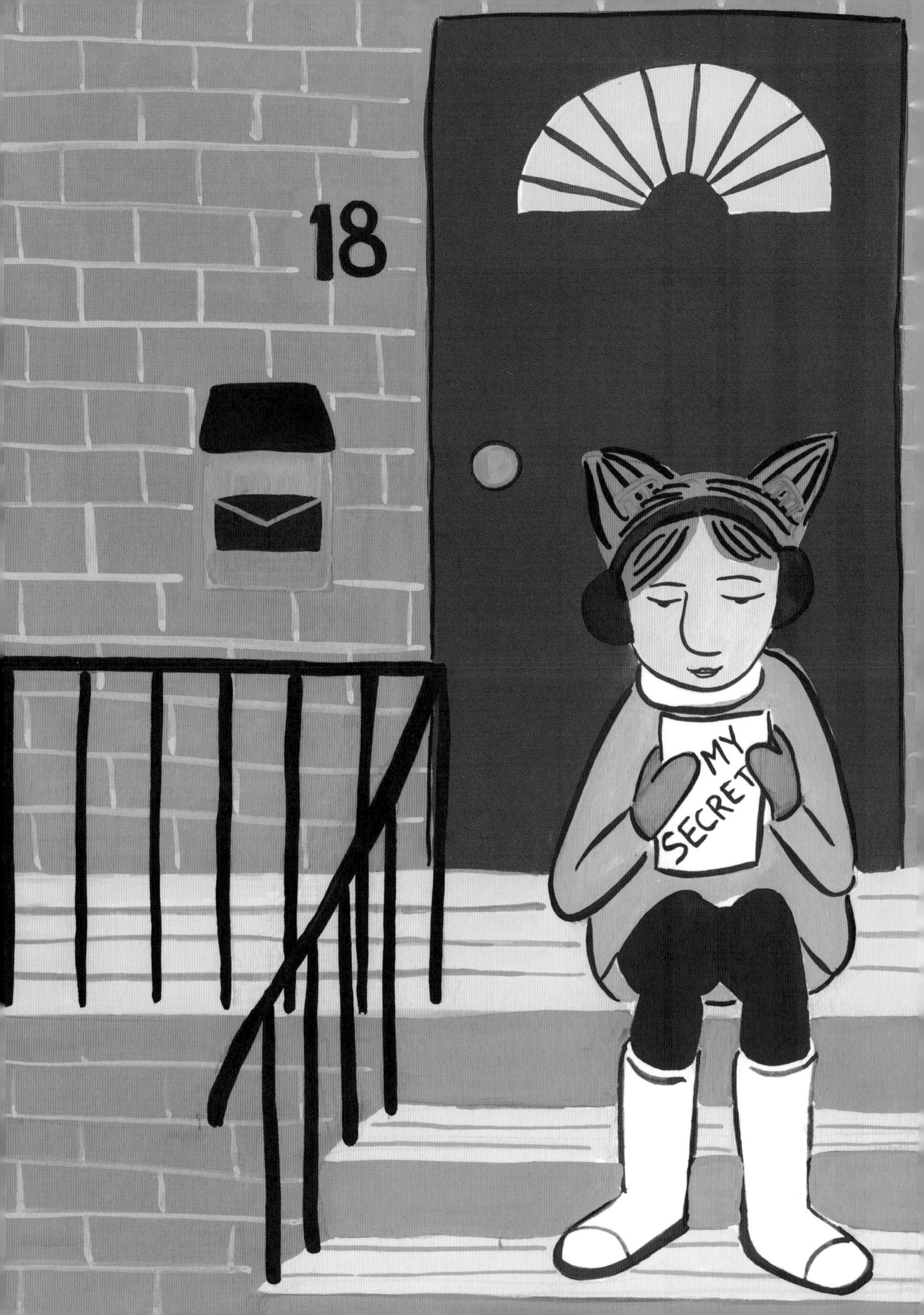
18
MY SECRET

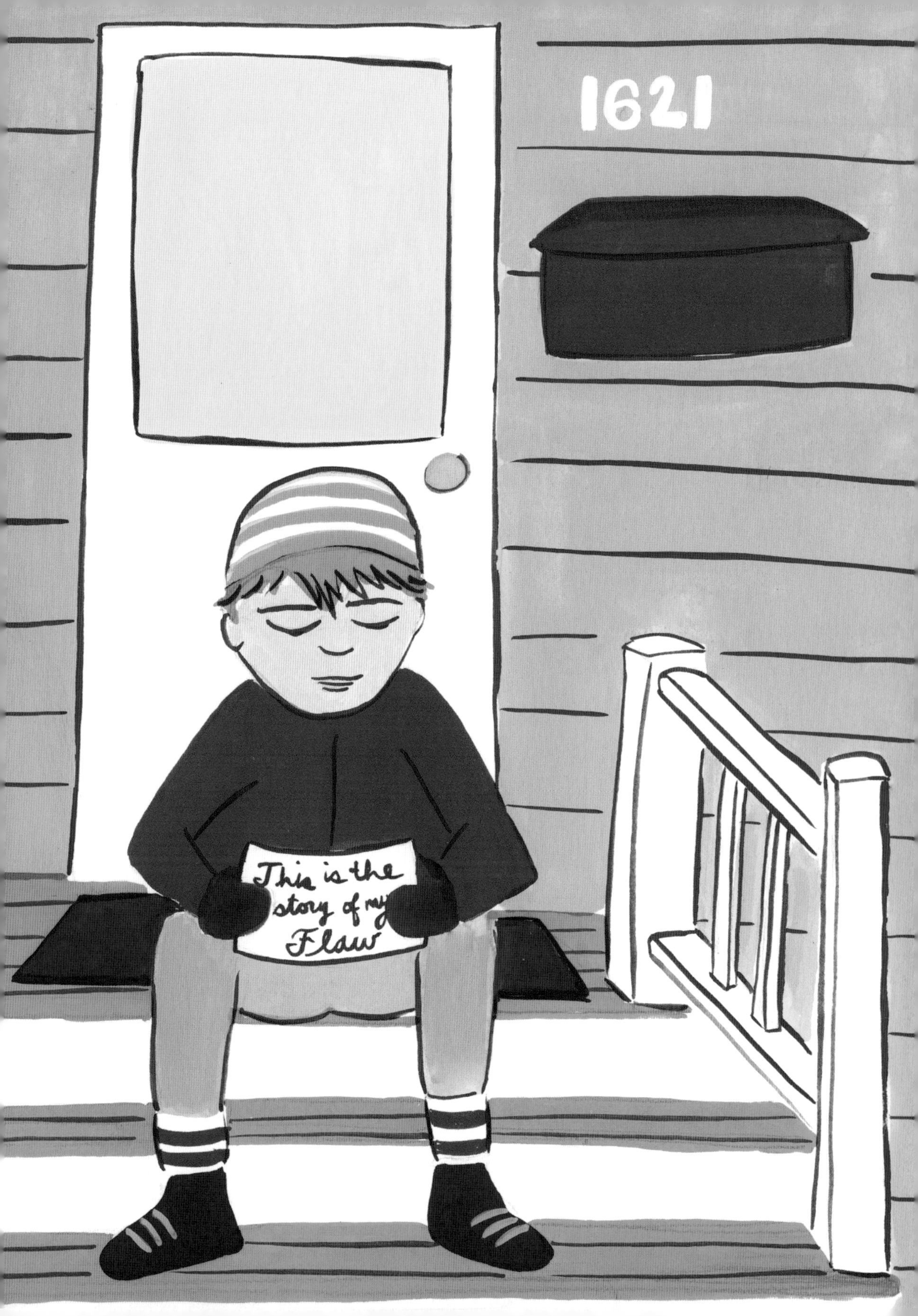
1621
This is the story of my Flaw

I can't tell you what Dave's secret was because it's his to tell. I will say that I was surprised he was afraid to tell me. It didn't seem like a big deal, but I'm not Dave.

"I love your secret postcard," I told him.

"I was embarrassed to tell you," he said.

"I think it's really brave you told me."

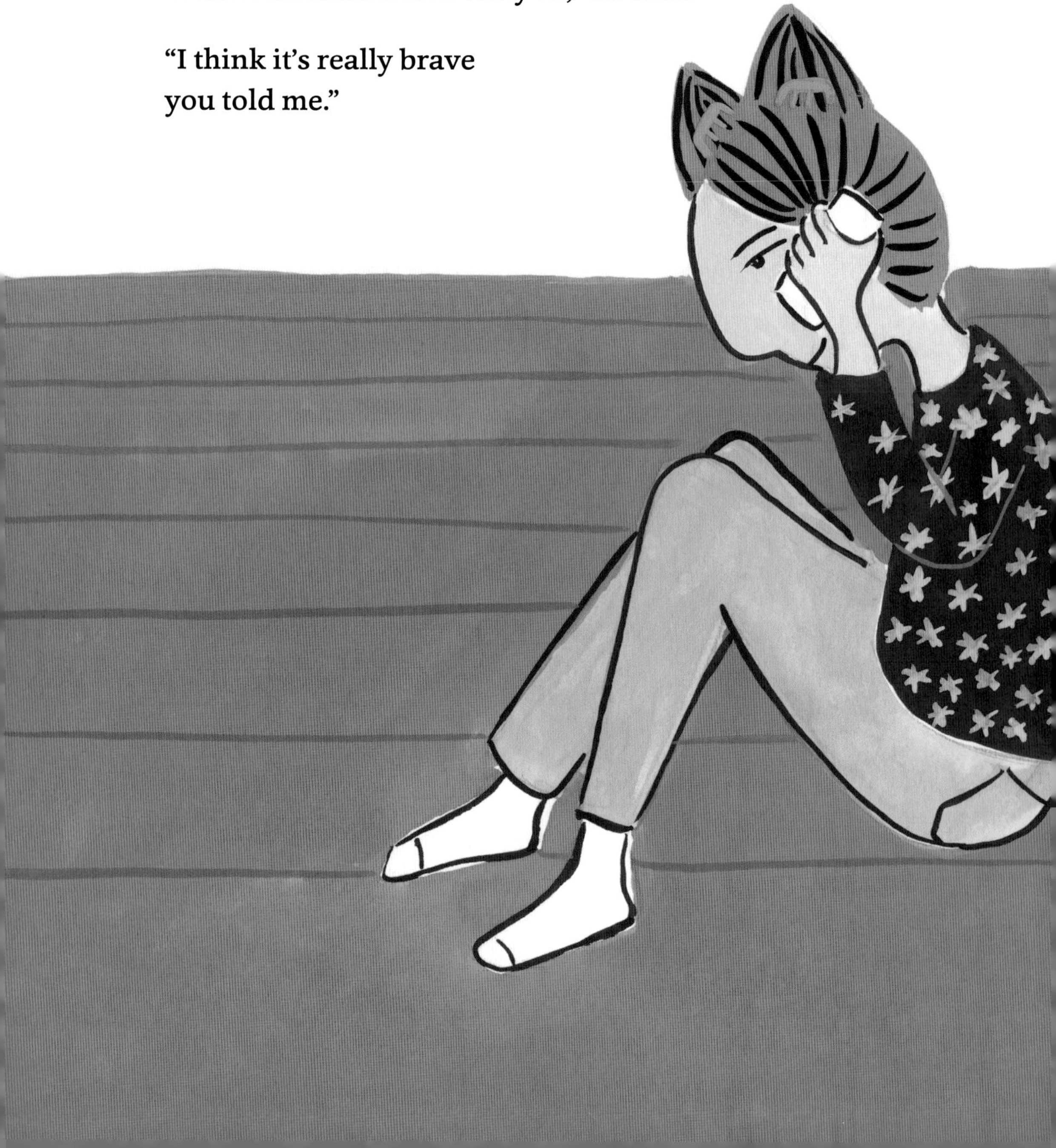

"Thanks," he said with an unfamiliar shyness.
"I read your postcard too."

I held my breath.

"It was beautiful."

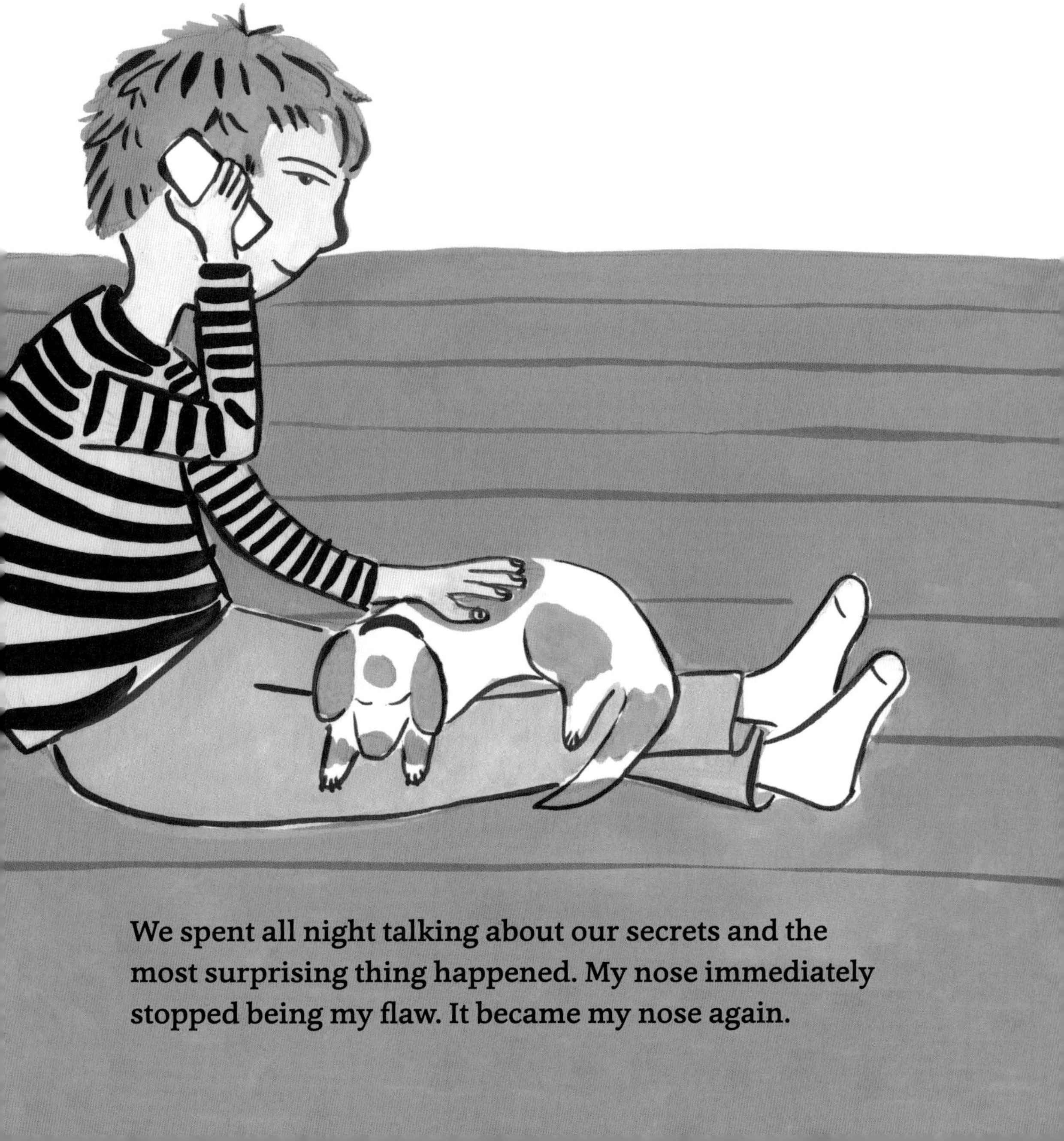

We spent all night talking about our secrets and the most surprising thing happened. My nose immediately stopped being my flaw. It became my nose again.

Something else happened. We *really* started to get to know each other.

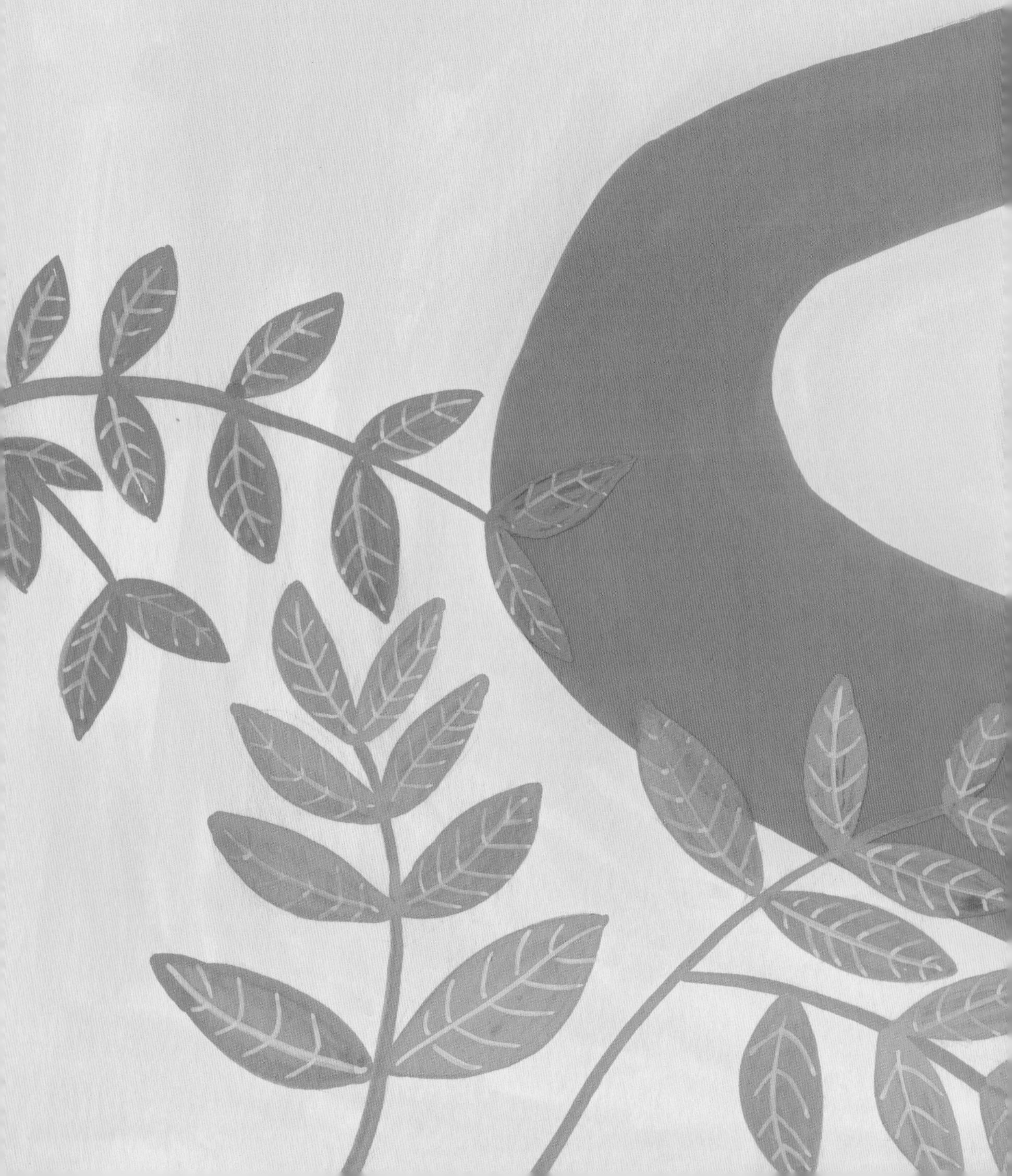

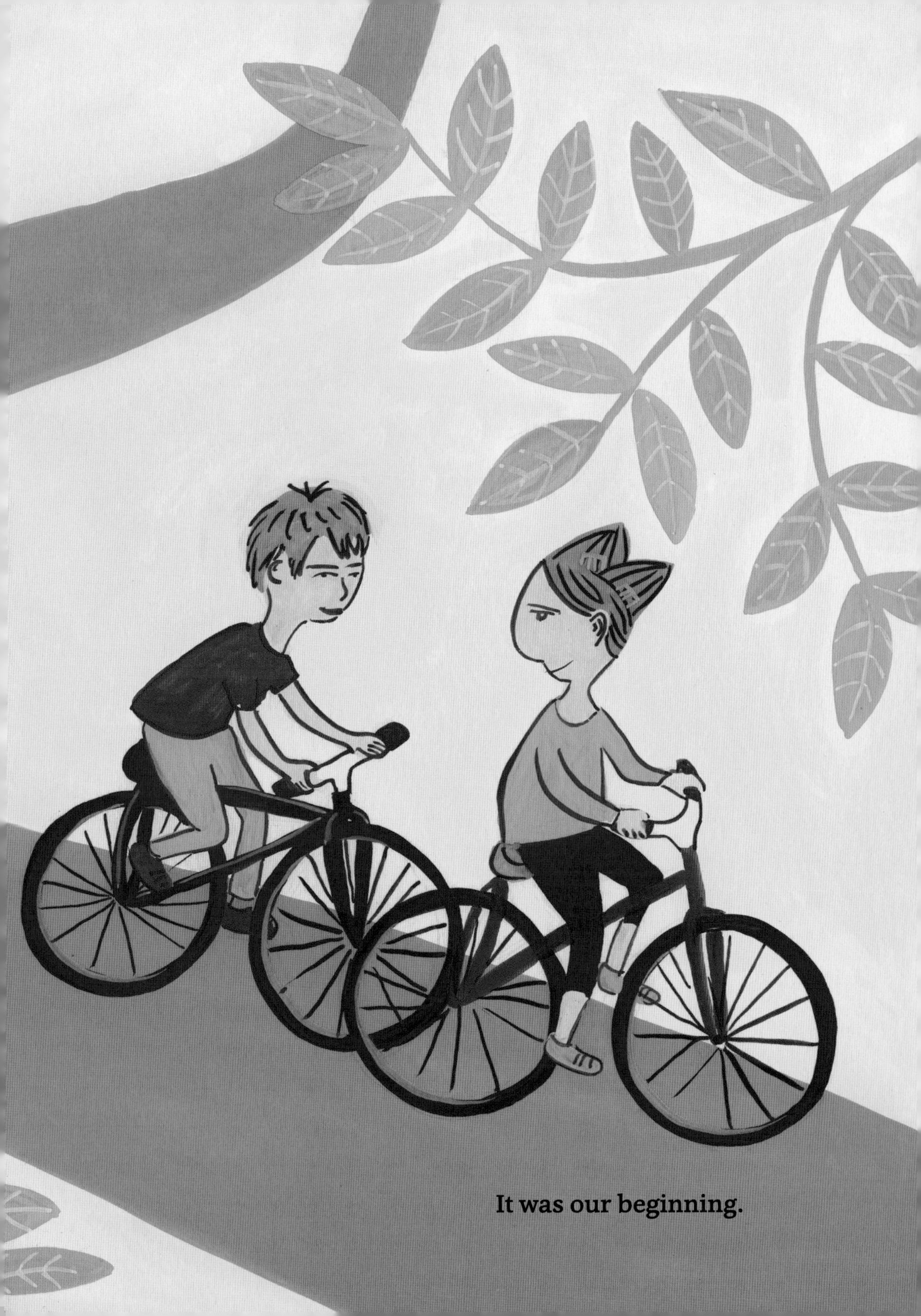

It was our beginning.

A few years later Dave told me about a mother who wanted to have her daughter's ears pinned back so she would fit in better at school.

He asked the girl what she thought of her ears. She said she liked them a lot. Dave told her he liked them too.

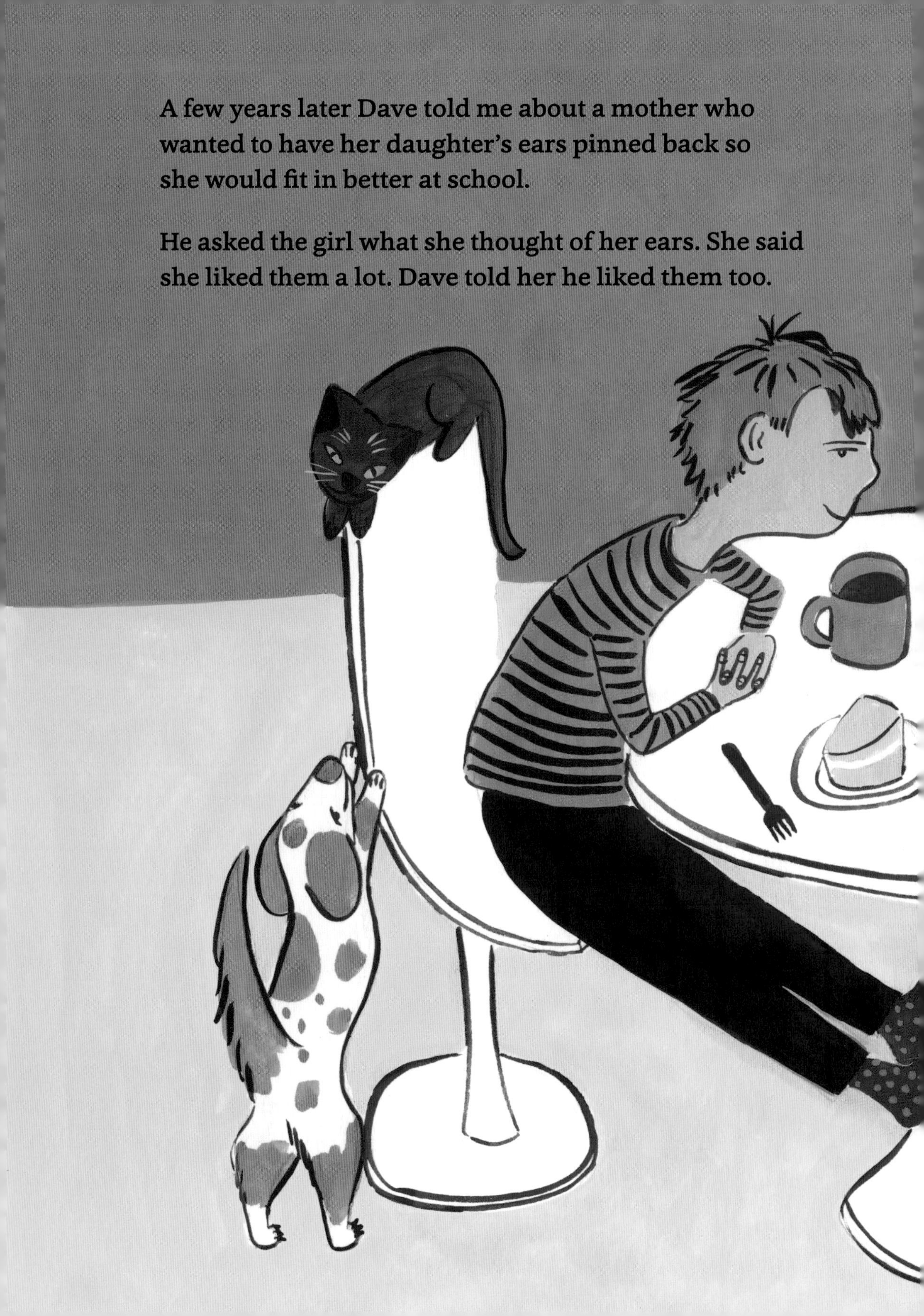

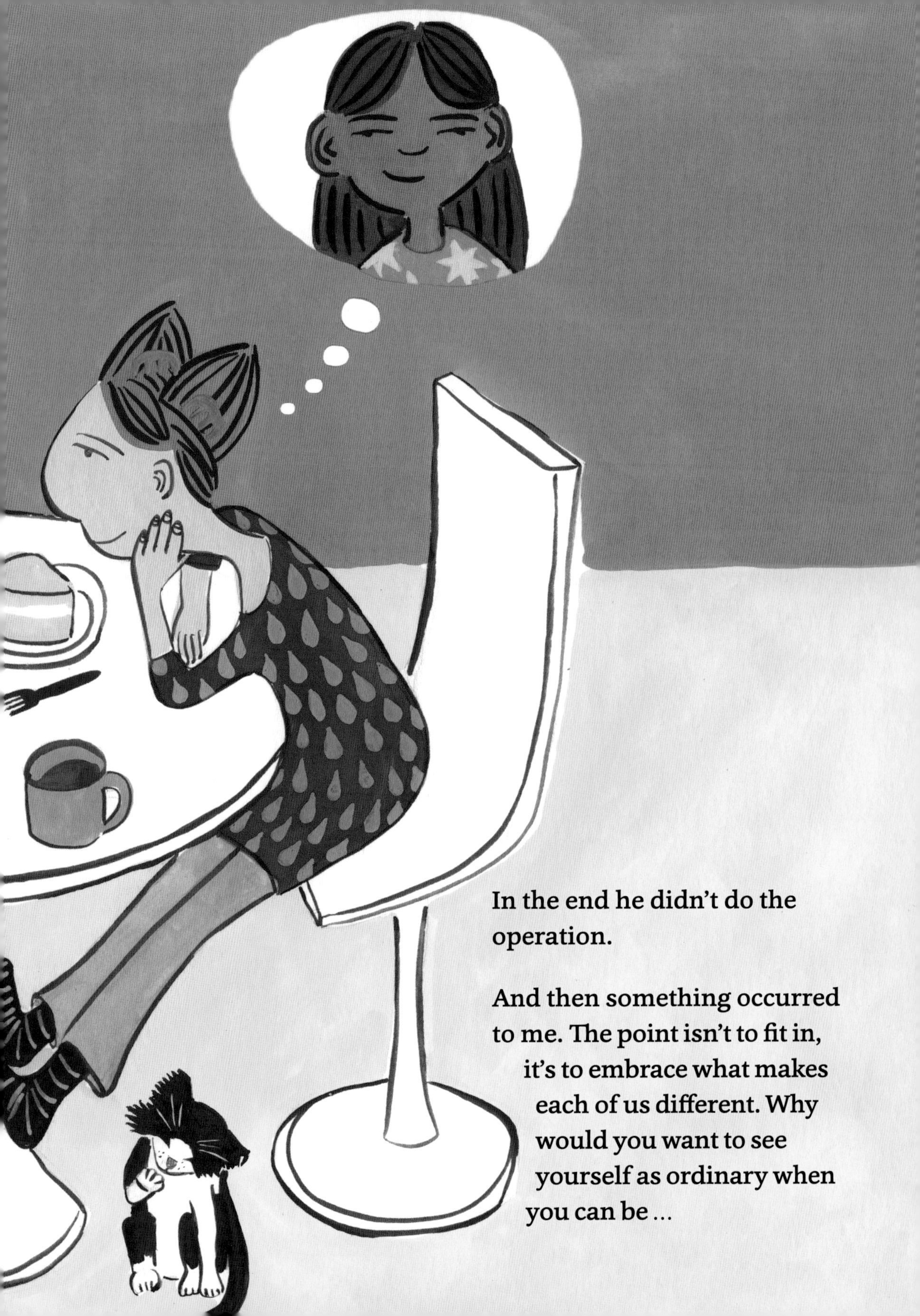

In the end he didn't do the operation.

And then something occurred to me. The point isn't to fit in, it's to embrace what makes each of us different. Why would you want to see yourself as ordinary when you can be ...

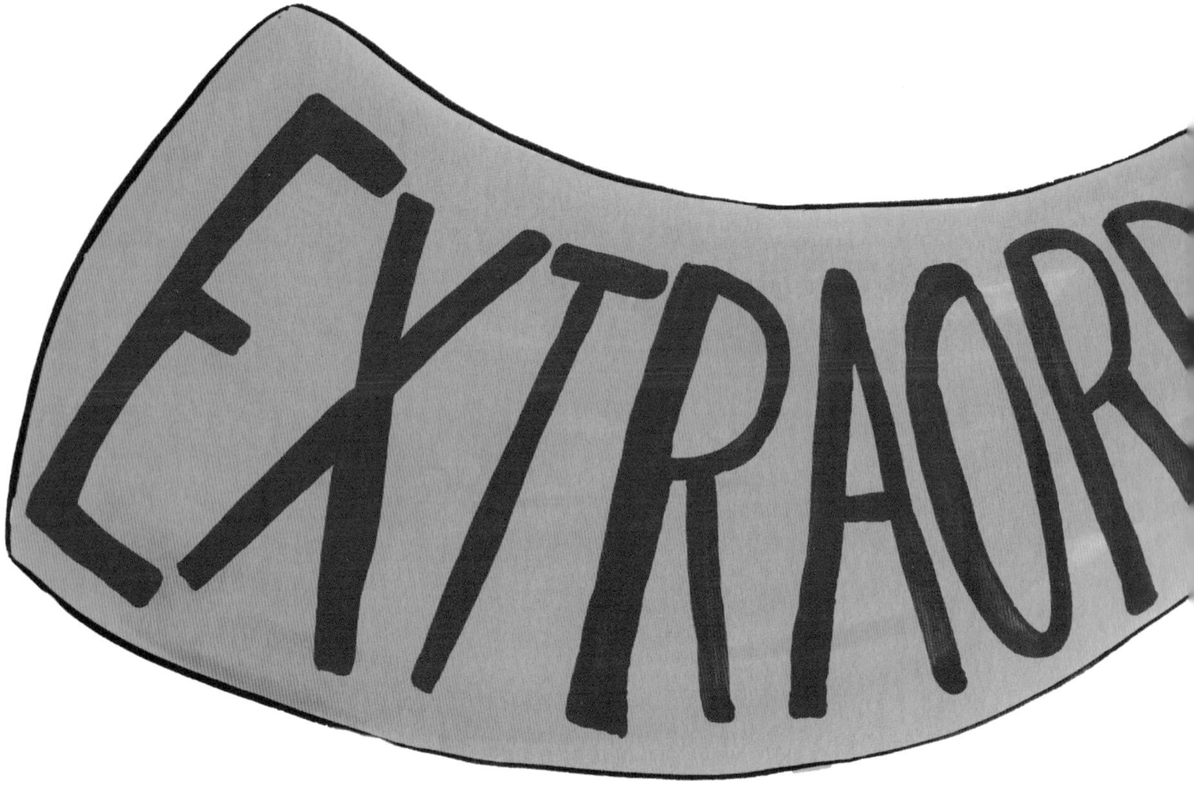
EXTRAOR

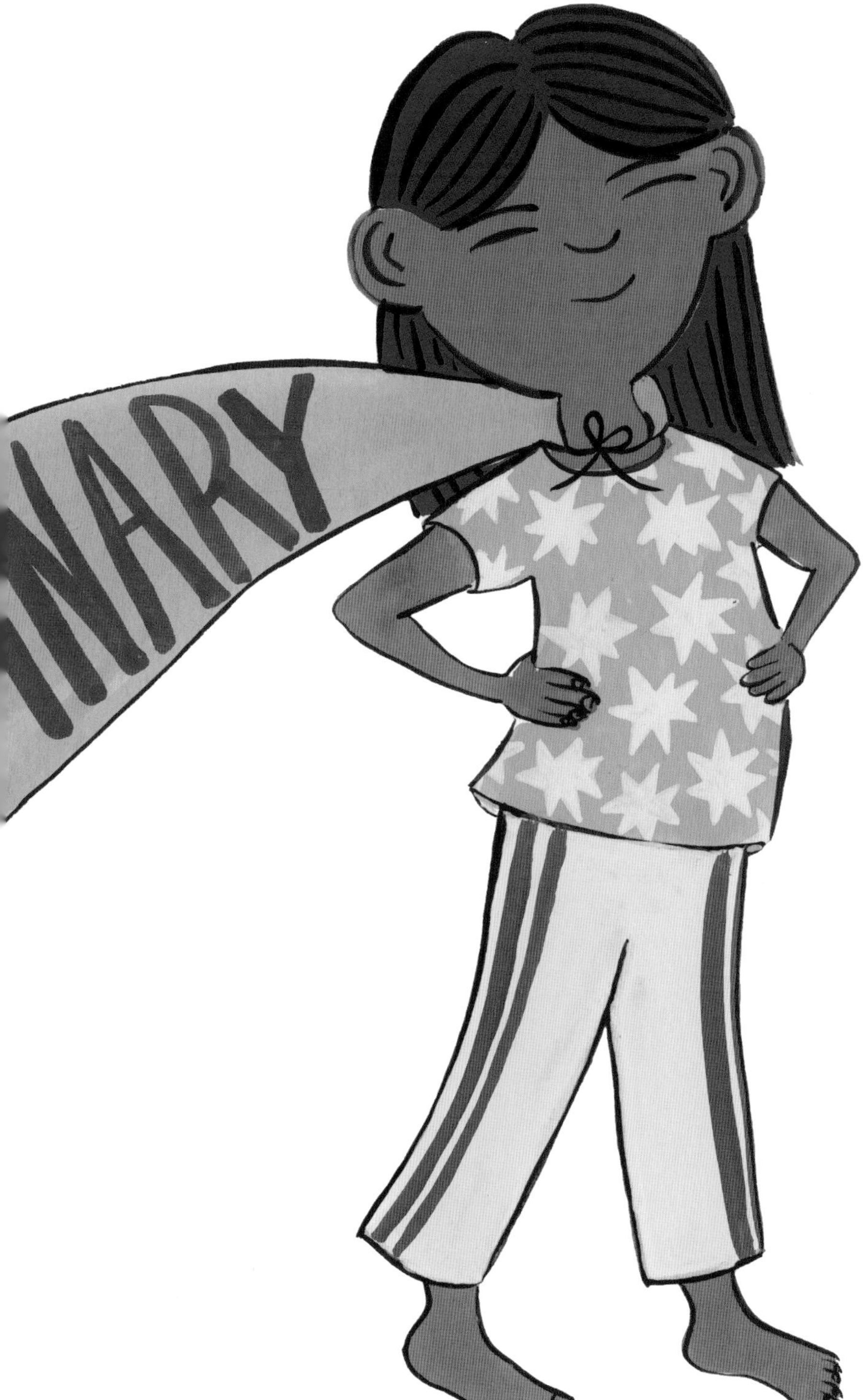
NARY

Author's Notebook

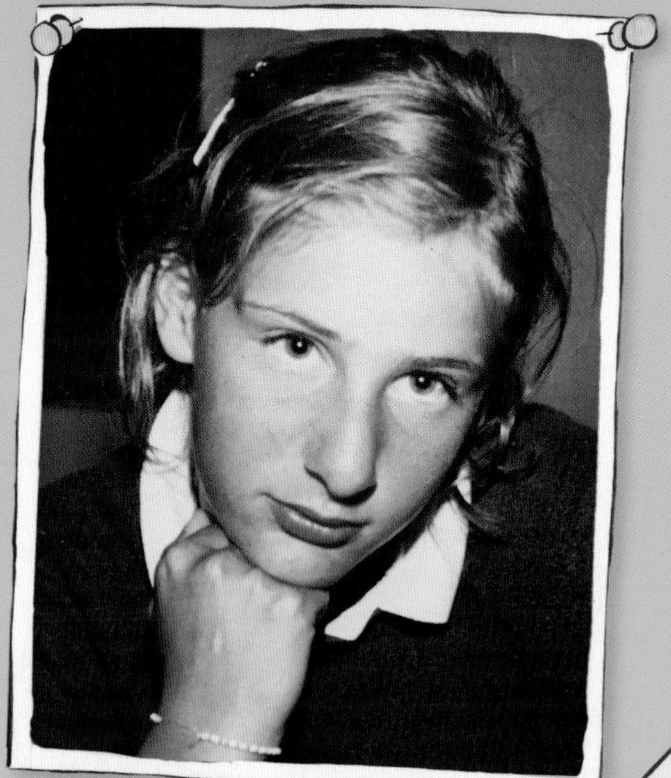

Andrea, age 14

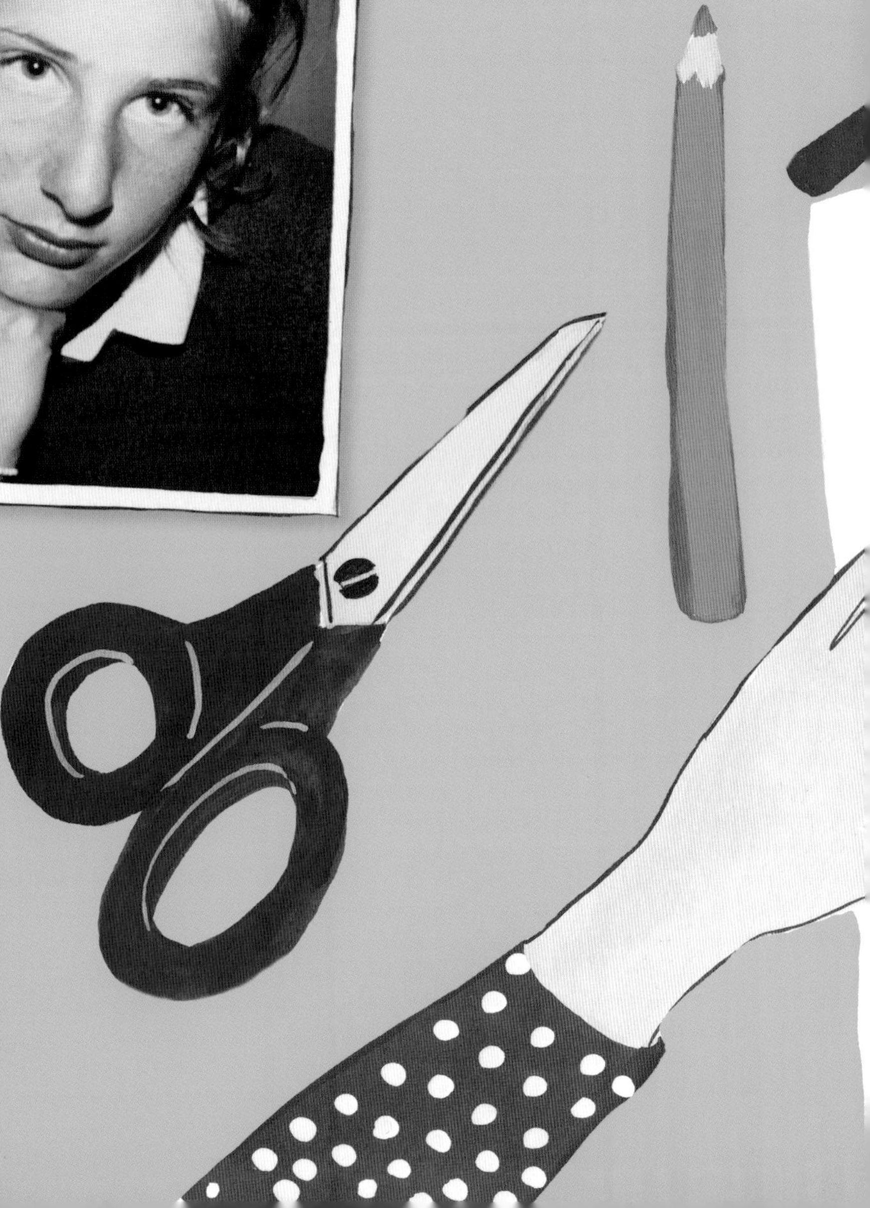

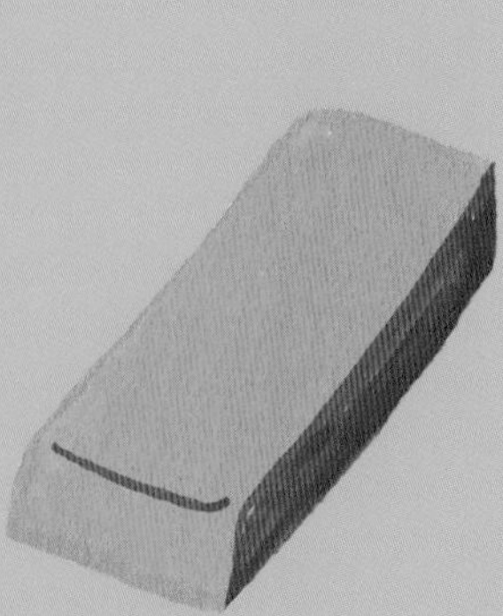

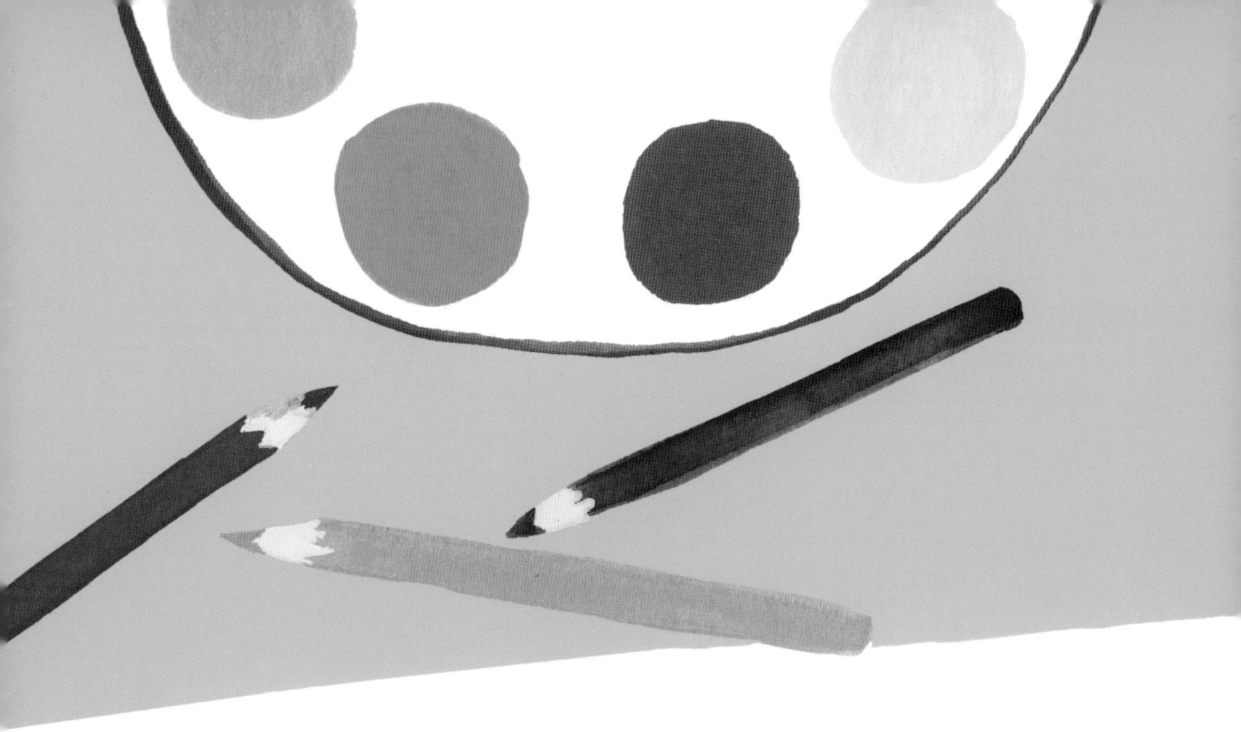

Hi! You just read a true story from my life! Let me tell you a little about how this story came to be.

I was born in Toronto and, like most kids, I loved art — especially painting and drawing. When I was 9 I was given my first camera and I completely fell in love with taking photos. Then when I was 12 my Dad passed along his old Super 8 movie camera to me. I made quirky, experimental films with my friends and we'd gather around the movie projector to watch them. Telling stories through motion pictures was magic.

Eventually I moved from Toronto to Halifax to attend art college, and after graduation I got a job working in the camera department of a movie studio that makes big commercial films. Eventually I tried my hand at directing my own films. I made lots of shorts and a couple of features and documentaries, but all that time I missed painting and drawing. When I started experimenting with illustration for my films, I quickly discovered that animation was the perfect marriage of my two loves: filmmaking and painting. I eventually moved back to Toronto but continued to work in Halifax now and again. On one such trip back in the summer of 2006, I met and fell in love with Dave.

Flawed was first presented as a time-lapse film that I made for the National Film Board of Canada in 2010. By then Dave and I were living in Halifax together, as we still do today. We have two cats, Pippa and Archie, and a dog, Sophie. Dave's kids, Max and Sydney, live with us part of the time. And I'm still painting and making films.

Over the next few pages you'll see some of the actual postcards Dave and I sent to each other, stills from my film, *Flawed*, and pictures of us today.

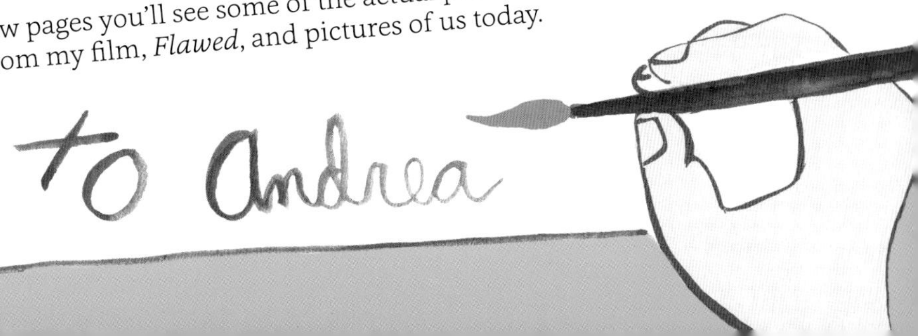
to Andrea

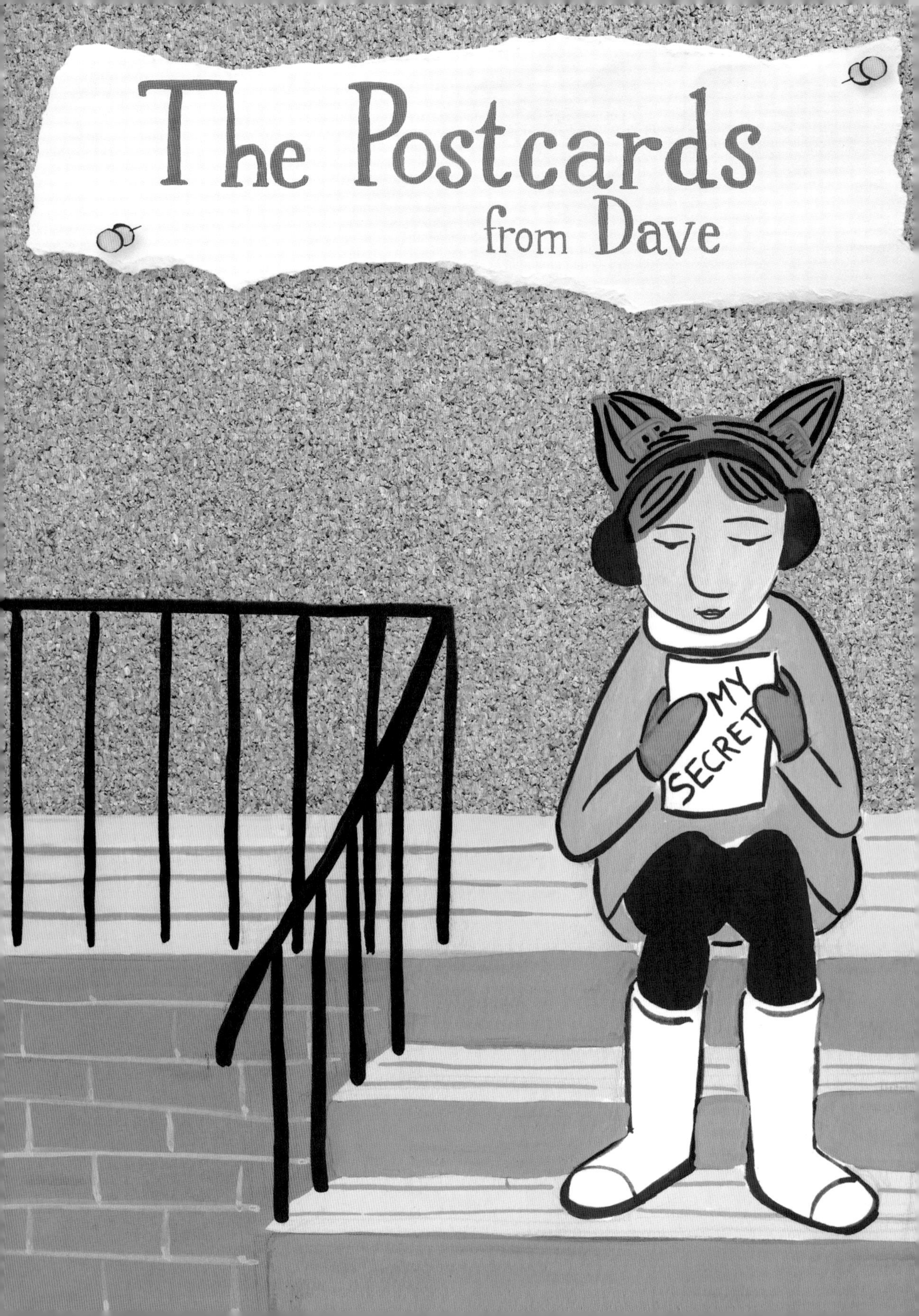
The Postcards
from Dave
MY SECRET

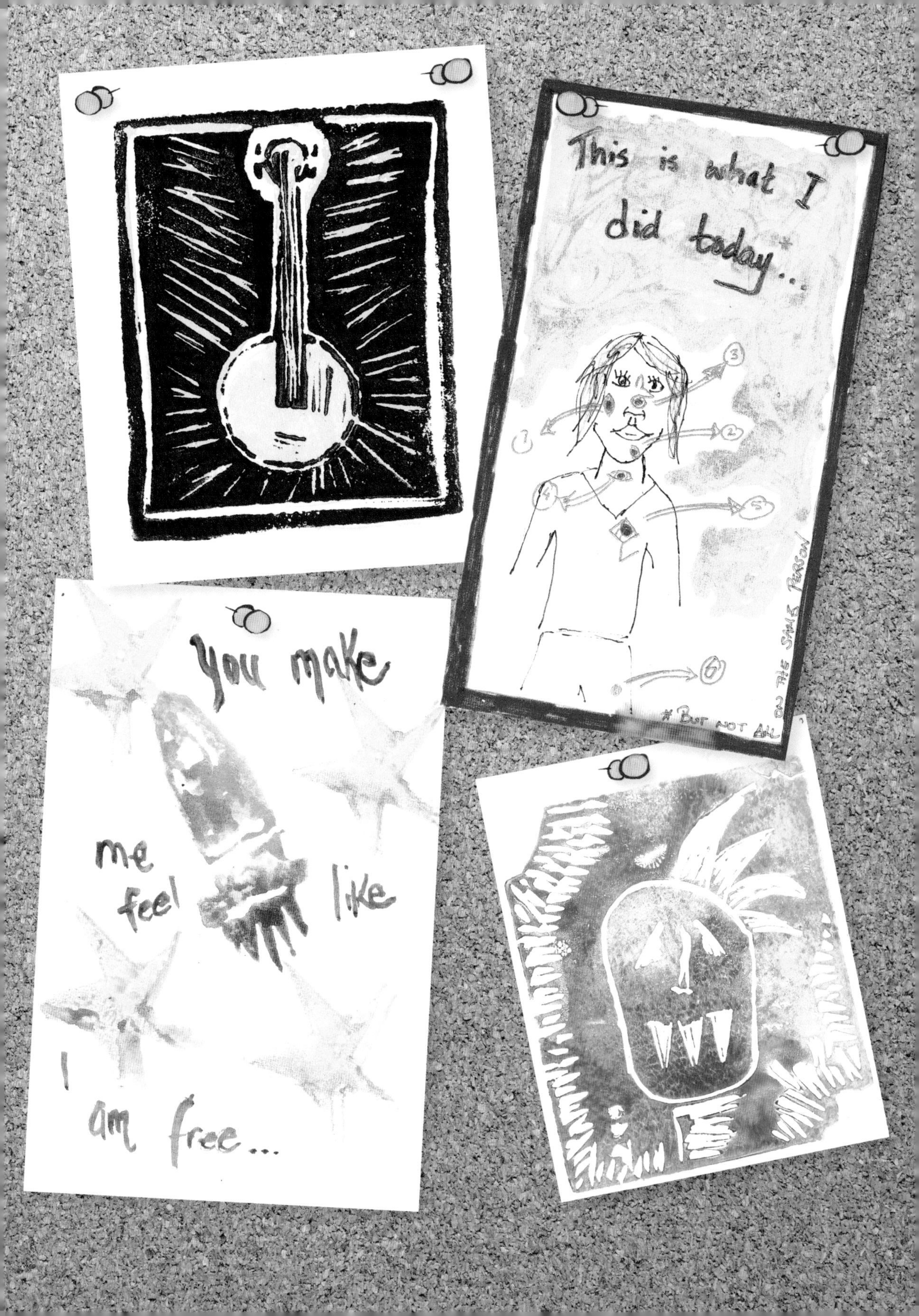
This is what I did today*...
1
2
3
4
5
6
*But not all on the same person
You make me feel like I am free...

The Postcards from Andrea

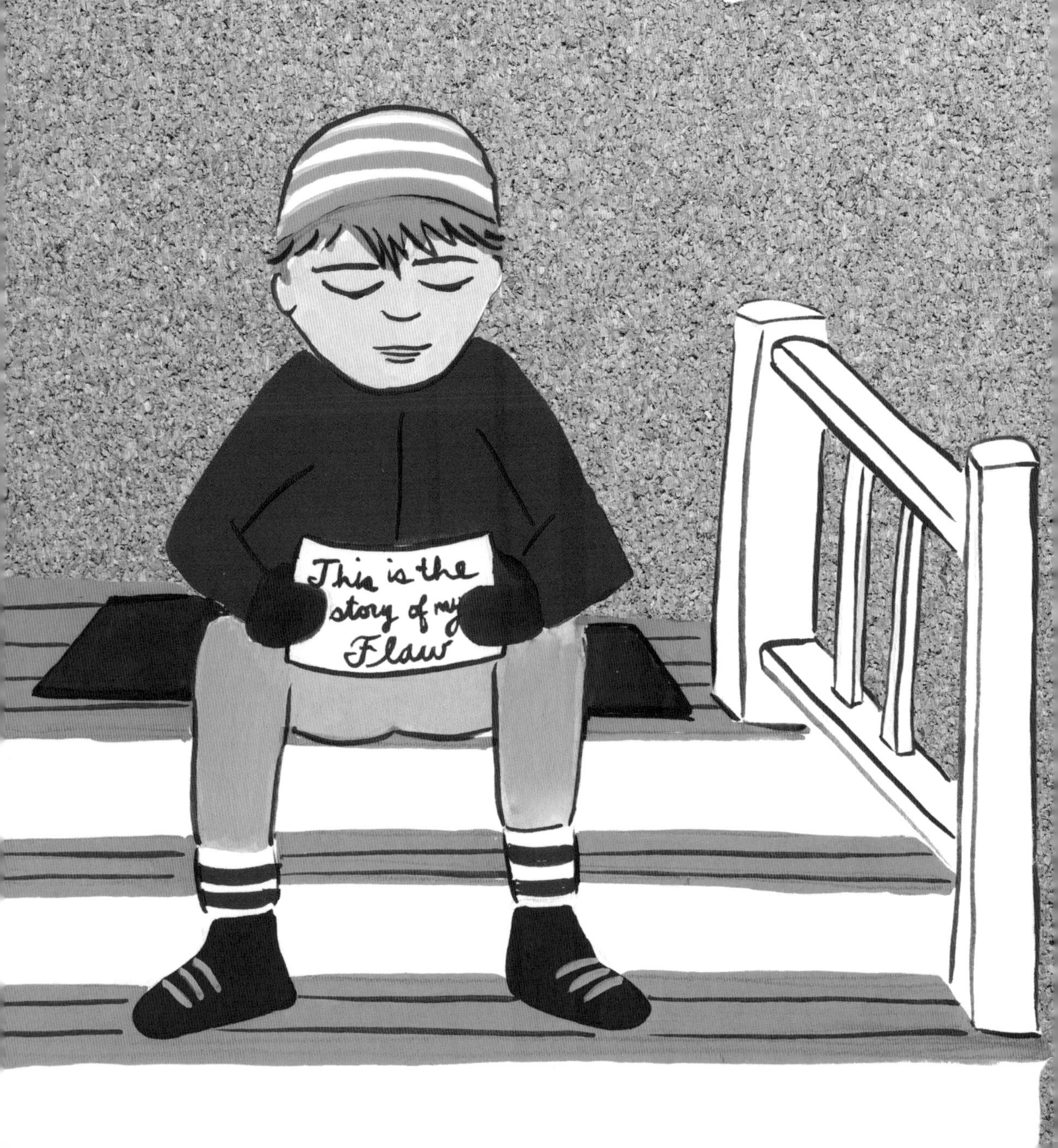

This is the story of my Flaw

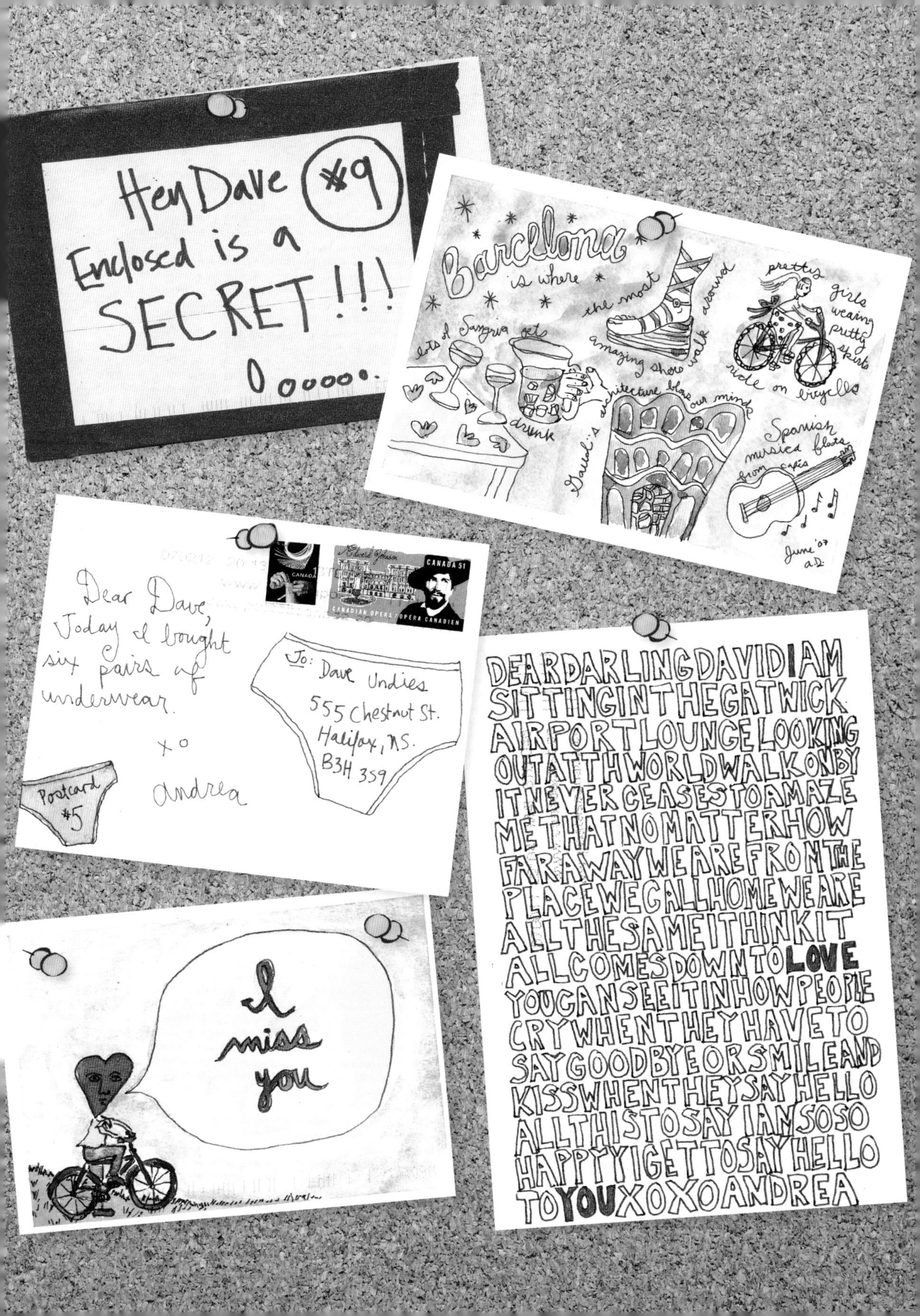
Hey Dave #9
Enclosed is a
SECRET!!!
Ooooo..
Barcelona is where
lots of Sangria gets drunk
the most amazing shoes walk around
pretty girls wearing pretty skirts ride on bicycles
Gaudi's architecture blows our minds
Spanish musica floats from cafés
June '07 a.D.
Dear Dave,
Today I bought six pairs of underwear.
xo
andrea
Postcard #5
CANADA
CANADA 51
CANADIAN OPERA / OPÉRA CANADIEN
To: Dave Undies
555 Chestnut St.
Halifax, NS.
B3H 3S9
DEARDARLINGDAVIDIAM
SITTINGINTHEGATWICK
AIRPORTLOUNGELOOKING
OUTATTHWORLDWALKONBY
ITNEVERCEASESTOAMAZE
METHATNOMATTERHOW
FARAWAYWEAREFROMTHE
PLACEWECALLHOMEWEARE
ALLTHESAMEITHINKIT
ALLCOMESDOWNTOLOVE
YOUCANSEEITINHOWPEOPLE
CRYWHENTHEYHAVETO
SAYGOODBYEORSMILEAND
KISSWHENTHEYSAYHELLO
ALLTHISTOSAYIAMSOSO
HAPPYIGETTOSAYHELLO
TOYOUXOXOANDREA
I miss you

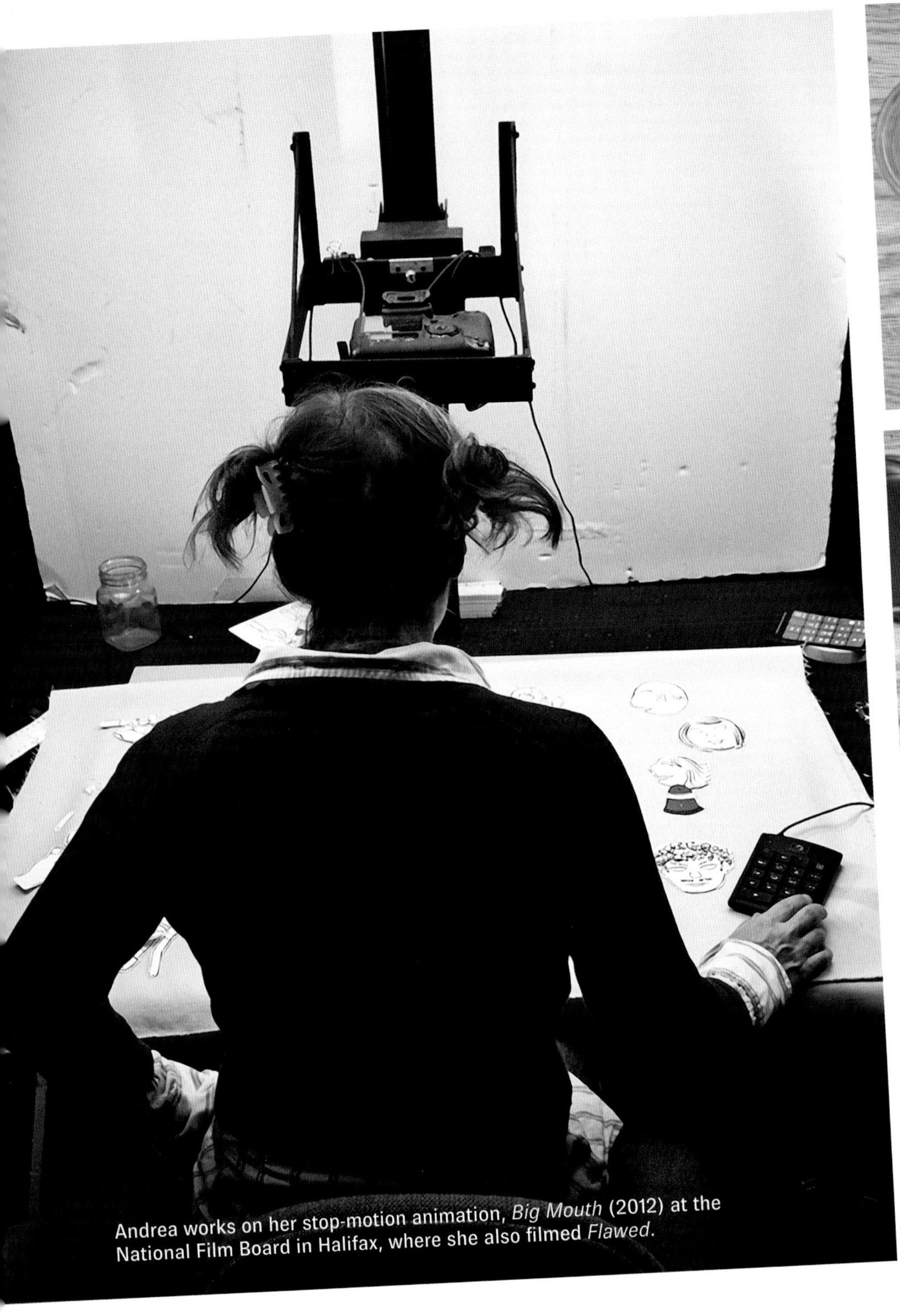

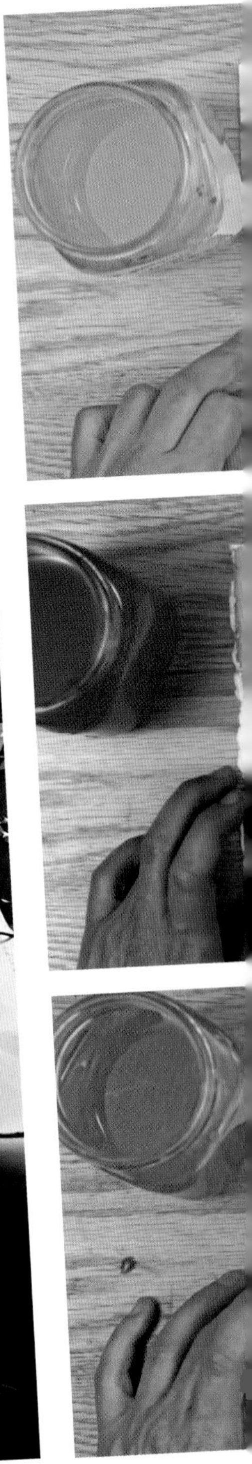

Andrea works on her stop-motion animation, *Big Mouth* (2012) at the National Film Board in Halifax, where she also filmed *Flawed*.

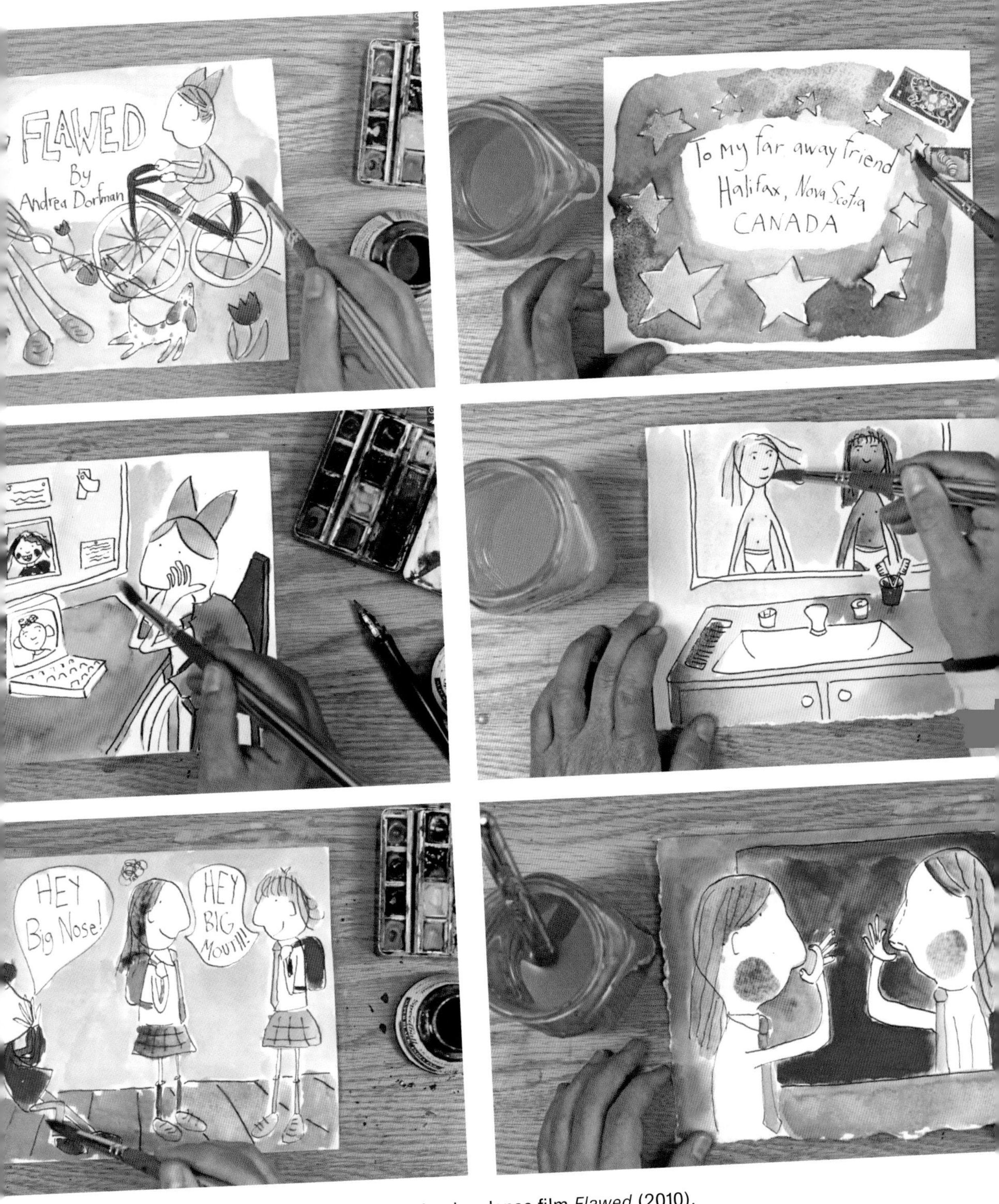
FLAWED
By
Andrea Dorfman
To my far away friend
Halifax, Nova Scotia
CANADA
HEY
Big Nose!
HEY
BIG
MOUTH!!

Stills from the time-lapse film *Flawed* (2010).

for Dave

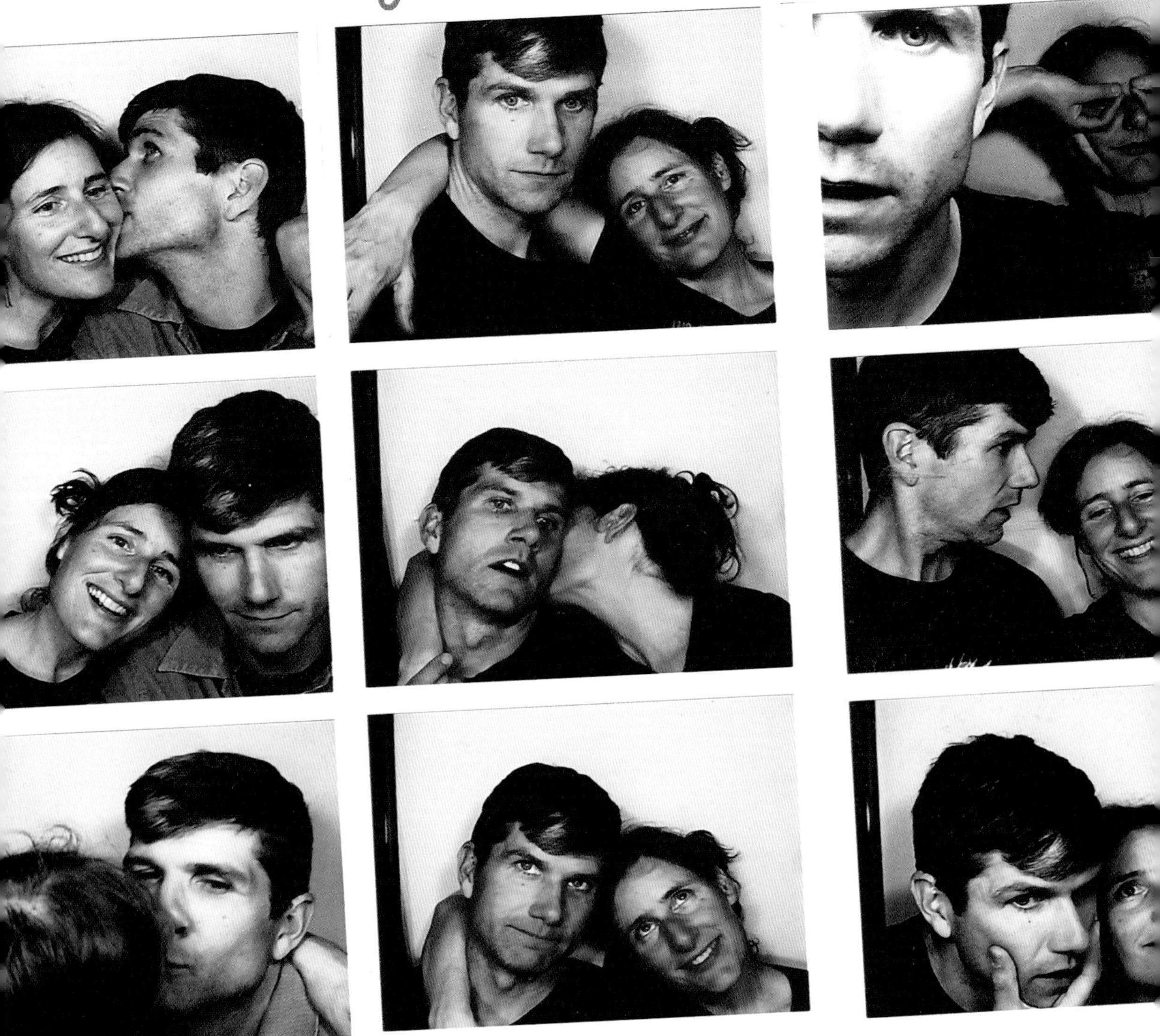

Making books and films isn't something you do alone, and since *Flawed* started as a film and THEN was made into a book, there are lots of people to thank. Thank you to everyone at Firefly Books and especially Steve Cameron, my editor, whose insights and ideas helped elevate this book. Thanks also to designer Hartley Millson for helping make the book version of *Flawed* a beautiful work of art. Thank you to everyone at the National Film Board of Canada for supporting me in creating the original film and especially Annette Clarke, my fearless producer and friend, for all of her creative input and general enthusiasm for my work. Thank you to Max and Sydney for all of the arts and crafts at the dining room table; your passion for creating was a well of inspiration for me to draw on throughout the making of *Flawed* and other films. And of course thank you to Dave. Without him, there would be no *Flawed*.